The Measurement of Urban Home Environment

VALIDATION AND STANDARDIZATION OF THE MINNESOTA HOME STATUS INDEX

By

ALICE M. LEAHY

Associate Professor, School of Social Work, Catholic University
Formerly Lecturer in the Department of Sociology and Social Work
and Research Worker in the Institute of Child Welfare
University of Minnesota

GREENWOOD PRESS, PUBLISHERS
WESTPORT, CONNECTICUT

Library of Congress Cataloging in Publication Data

Leahy, Alice Mary, 1891-
    The measurement of urban home environment.

    Reprint of the 1936 ed. published by the University
of Minnesota Press, Minneapolis, which was issued as
no. 11 of the series: University of Minnesota. The
Institute of Child Welfare. Monograph series.
    Bibliography: p.
    Includes index.
    1. Social classes. 2. Home. I. Title.
II. Series: Minnesota. University. Institute of
Child Development and Welfare. Monograph series ;
no. 11.
HT611.L4 1975   301.44   79-142314
ISBN 0-8371-5902-4

HT
611·
L4

Originally published in 1936 by the University of Minnesota
Press, Minneapolis

Reprinted in 1975 by Greenwood Press, Inc.,
51 Riverside Avenue, Westport, Conn. 06880

Library of Congress catalog card number 79-142314
ISBN 0-8371-5902-4

Printed in the United States of America

10 9 8 7 6 5 4 3 2

FOREWORD

Sometimes a scientist, engaged with a major problem, finds it necessary to develop a new measuring instrument. Such an instrument, a by-product in a sense, often becomes a device by means of which other problems can be attacked and thus acquires a value that is independent of the original investigation for which it was evolved. Many great advances, both practical and scientific, have been made in this way.

The derivation and standardization of such an instrument is described in this monograph. In a study of the development of children in foster homes, Dr. Leahy was under the necessity of securing an objective means of giving quantitative expression to differences in home and cultural environment. This problem with its many difficulties is one with which many workers in the field of sociology and child welfare have been concerned. After a brief summary of these attempts, Dr. Leahy shows how the Minnesota Home Status Index, developed with care and precision by means of modern statistical techniques, brings this problem nearer its solution.

Such a scale, in addition to its scientific value, may be of much practical value to social and child welfare workers, since it affords a method of evaluating the home and cultural environment that is dependent not upon casual impression but rather upon carefully recorded observations.

If the final form of the instrument here described in detail fulfills its promise in giving us a more complete understanding of the child in his social setting, Dr. Leahy will be well repaid for the energy and care put into its construction.

JOHN E. ANDERSON
Director, Institute of Child Welfare

ACKNOWLEDGMENTS

The writer is greatly indebted to the parents and children who cooperated in this study and to the respective directors of the Institute of Child Welfare of the University of Minnesota, the St. Lawrence Parochial School, the North East Neighborhood House, and Pillsbury Settlement House for their kindness in assisting in the location of the experimental population.

Grateful acknowledgment is made also of the helpful criticisms and suggestions offered by Dr. Florence L. Goodenough and Dr. F. Stuart Chapin.

To Dr. John E. Anderson, director of the Institute of Child Welfare of the University of Minnesota, sincere appreciation is expressed for his encouragement, able criticism, and guidance throughout the study.

TABLE OF CONTENTS

I. INTRODUCTION

THE PROBLEM

Although students of human behavior have for a long time stressed the significance of the child's environment in shaping his conduct, relatively few instruments have been devised with which one may measure that environment. The complexity of environment makes the problem of measurement an exceedingly difficult one. This study does not undertake to set up a device sensitive enough to measure the psychological attributes of environment. Such an instrument must await reliable measures of human personality, for indeed human personality is the stuff of which the psychological aspects of environment are made. An instrument for measuring the physical situation in which conduct takes place is entirely feasible, however. Conceding the limited predictive value of such a device for any one individual, valuable comparisons of a given individual's environment with the prevailing standard may be made. Further, its use for large groups of children is clear. Without it, judgments of the relationship of behavior and physical environment are made on the basis of isolated incidents, fads, or pet theories. To illustrate: Delinquency and poverty are presumed to be coexistent; but of what does poverty consist? to what extent do the homes and neighborhoods of delinquents differ from those of children in general? If the theory that intelligence is directly related to socio-economic status is valid, an objective measure of the latter is necessary. Because it is possible to group children into homogeneous intellectual groups in the schoolroom, it is frequently concluded that they have equal opportunities to learn. But how do cultural facilities in the home contribute to the child's performance? Are his extra-school experiences richer than those of other children? The fact that a home equals or surpasses the general average of homes in cultural facilities, such as newspapers, reference books, and concert attendance, is significant for the interpretation of the conduct of a bright boy who scorns and resists formal schooling. In the field of foster home placement, the value of objective measures of environment for judging the relative level of a home needs no elaboration. Instruments for measuring physical and mental traits protect foster homes against defective children. Should not

1

foster children be placed with greater awareness of the extent to which the proposed home deviates from the generality?

Certainly the practical problems of child training demand that the factors constituting the child's environment be isolated and measured. In the field of theory, no less an issue than the nature-nurture problem, which has challenged investigators for several decades, awaits reliable measures of environment. The problem of describing environmental differences demands recognition of two facts: first, that there are many institutions in the child's environment — the community, the church, the playground, the school, and the home; and, secondly, that each institution has its own particular qualitative and objective characteristics.

An instrument that would attempt to measure all the institutions in an individual's environment would be one of unreasonable length and unwieldiness. The most important institution is unquestionably the home, for it is the home that influences the child's conduct most continuously. As we have said, the objective characteristics of an institution are obviously the most easily and reliably measured. And although they provide only the structural framework, they are basic and essential parts of the qualitative fabric of a situation. The techniques developed range from an evaluation of a single factor to the statistical analysis of a number of elements.

PREVIOUS STUDIES

Single indices of environmental differences. — Most investigators regard occupation as the best single index to differences between homes. In 1913 Taussig (39) proposed a classification of five non-competing occupational groups. Day laborers, who must have great bodily strength but need little or no education, constitute his lowest group. The semiskilled workman is placed in the second group. The skilled workman, who must have a small amount of education as well as brawn, is in the third group. Taussig also assumes that material possessions differentiate this group from the two lower ones. His fourth group includes office managers and clerical and semiprofessional workers. Well-to-do professional and business men are placed in the fifth, or highest, group. Because of the specific attributes of education, savings, and property that Taussig attached to each occupational category, his classification scheme has had only a limited applicability. In actual practice only the learned professions have definite educational requirements. In 1918 Barr (2) constructed a scale in which one hundred occupations were assigned values according to judges' estimates of the relative demands made on intelligence by each occupation. The limited number of occupations considered restricts the usefulness of this scale.

Other social scientists, notably Terman (40), Counts (13), Anderson (21), and Goodenough (21), have offered occupational classifications based on census figures which have had wide usefulness. The scale of Goodenough and Anderson (21), published by the Institute of Child Welfare of the University of Minnesota, incorporates the ideas of both Taussig and Barr. It follows the census figures and distributes the occupations into noncompeting groups classified according to the relative demands made on mental ability.

Attempts to measure family life from the standpoint of income have been made by several investigators. Engel's study (16) was the first to demonstrate the need of recognizing the composition of the family (size, age, and sex) in devising a unit for interpreting income. This unit, the "quet," * he defined as the cost of maintenance of the individual at birth. He postulated that the cost of maintenance increases 0.10 quet a year to the age of twenty-five years in men and twenty years in women. Although these values are entirely arbitrary and without validation, Engel's study represents clearly the impossibility of regarding gross income as sufficient to determine "effective income."

In all probability the most exhaustive studies of income as an index of the economic level of the home have been made by Sydenstricker and his associates (35–37). Following the dietary studies of Atwater (1), who expressed the caloric food requirements of persons of different sexes and ages in terms of the requirements of adult males, Sydenstricker developed two indices for measuring family living conditions. One he called the Fammain Scale, the other the Ammain Scale. The former, which is an abbreviation for "food expense for adult male maintenance," lists the relative cost of food for persons of different sexes and ages. It was determined from the records of food supplies for fifteen hundred families. The Ammain Scale, "adult male maintenance," represents the monetary cost of food, clothing, and miscellaneous individual requirements combined. It presumes to express so far as possible the relative differences between various economic needs and was determined on the basis of complete budgets for 140 families over a twelve-month period. The procedure for using the scales is the same. The monthly family income is divided by the number of units in the family. The quotient

---

* In honor of Quetelet.

is the family's monthly income per unit. Thus, any family, or group of families, for which the total income and the sex and age of each member are known may be classified for comparative purposes. In the Ammain Scale, Sydenstricker has provided the most accurate single measure of economic status thus far constructed. Yet both his scales are distinctly limited in their application, since they were built solely from data for wage-earning families in South Carolina milling villages (1916–17).

The telephone was demonstrated by Kornhauser (26) to differentiate homes in his study of economic status in relation to intelligence of school children. The choice of the telephone was arbitrary and, like other single indices, permits very wide differences in respect to other factors. The educational, cultural, and social interests of a family are not revealed by the possession of a telephone.

Multiple factor classifications of environment. — In 1908 Commons (12) offered the first scheme demanding a consideration of more than a single factor in the classification of homes. His Score Card covered such features as the location of the house, congestion, lighting, structural condition, house appurtenances, number of occupants, sleeping arrangements, and cleanliness. Items requiring the judgment of the rater were included with more objective factors. To each, arbitrary weights were assigned. Although the plan was entirely empirical and without statistical validation, it is a forerunner of our modern scales.

Perry (33) incorporated in his measurement scheme, published in 1913, the concept of an environmental continuum for the objective features of home conditions. His Manner of Living Index, crude as it is, is significant in that it is our first scale for measuring environment. He assumes that the four basic processes undertaken in households are the preparation of food, eating, sleeping, and receiving friends; further, that these processes are carried on through the progressive acquisition of a kitchen, a bedroom, a dining room, and a living room. He weights household equipment in direct relationship to this progression. His method aimed at a clear demarcation of the different stages of household development. Unfortunately no statistical analysis was made, and the scale has been little used.

The next investigator to include several objective factors in measuring home differences was Holley (24), who published a study in 1916. In accordance with an arbitrary procedure he combined average education of parents, number of books in the home, and monthly rental into a single score. Using this index, he concludes that there is a high correlation between the economic, educational, and social advantages of a home and the number of years' schooling its children receive.

Chapman and Sims' study on "The Quantitative Measurement of Socio-Economic Status" (11), which was published in 1925, was the first of a series: Heilman's (23), Sims' (34), Chapin's (8), and McCormick's (28), all of which are noteworthy for the thorough statistical analysis that has been made of the data. The procedure used by Chapman and Sims involved reducing sixteen questions selected as indicative of socio-economic status to the "all or none" principle of possession or nonpossession. In the case of graduated traits, such as books and amount of schooling, possession was defined in arbitrary terms. Then, on the assumption that each trait was normally distributed, its value was expressed in terms of sigma deviations from the average of the group. The suitability of a given trait as a measure of socio-economic status was determined by the magnitude of its correlation with the total remaining traits and the smallness of its correlation with every other trait. Pearson's (32) biserial coefficient of correlation technique was used in establishing the former, and Yule's (46) coefficient of association was used for the latter. The final scale contains eleven items. Reliability, by the method of split halves and the Spearman-Brown formula, was found to be 0.77. The validity of the scale was not determined.

Undoubtedly the most widely used measurement of home environment is the Sims Score Card (34), adapted from the work of Chapman and Sims (11). As in the construction of the original instrument, a large population was used. In this instance, however, the survey covered the sixth, seventh, and eighth grades in schools whose children come from rich, from average, and from poor homes. The joint study, on the other hand, was limited to a high school population. Sims' final scale included 23 questions. The method of statistical analysis was similar to the original. Reliability, however, was raised to 0.91 by the split halves method, and one hundred paired siblings yielded a reliability of 0.95. Further improvement over the original work was made in the determination of validity. Two extreme occupational groups — the professional and the day labor groups — were found to be widely separated on the scale. Two selected neighborhoods that were generally considered far apart in social level were also distinctly contrasted when the scale was applied to their homes.

For the purposes of crude classification the Sims Score Card is of unquestioned usefulness. However, all three scales — the Sims (34), the Chapman-Sims (11), and the Heilman (23) — can be criticized on several counts. In the first place, too few aspects of the home are considered. Secondly, the scales use the questionnaire method and are dependent on information known to children. Thirdly, the data do not permit the use of the biserial coefficient of correlation, since their graduated character, as well as the matter of normal distribution, cannot be substantiated. Nor does the data fulfill the requirements assumed in the derivation of Yule's (46) coefficient of association, namely, a point nature.

Chapin (6) studied the problem of a quantitative measure of environment more intensively than any previous investigator. His Scale for Rating Living Room Equipment, published in 1928, was the culmination of an exhaustive consideration of several indices of home conditions. Defining socio-economic status as "the position that an individual or a family occupies with reference to the prevailing average standards of cultural possessions, effective income, material possessions, and participation in group activities of the community," he constructed scales to measure these four elements of family life. Under "cultural possessions" he listed classes of books and newspapers, musical instruments, and other articles, to which he gave arbitrary weights to form the culture score. "Material possessions" were similarly selected and weighted. The Ammain Scale of Sydenstricker was used to determine "effective income." A detailed record of membership, contributions, attendance, committee service, and official positions in clubs and community organizations formed the scale for "participation in group activity." Finding that the coefficients of intercorrelation between the four scales ranged from +.55 to +.68 and that the use of the entire four was an exceedingly lengthy task, Chapin selected 53 items from his Cultural Possessions and Material Possessions scales to form the Living Room Scale. It correlates +.56 to +.89 with the four original scales.

In the process of use and subsequent analysis, Chapin's Living Room Scale underwent considerable revision. The items known as "Built-in-Features" were found to occur so rarely as to be of little significance, and hence in 1930 this group was dropped. Later, in 1931, a group of items ("cleanliness," "orderliness," "condition of repair," and "visitor's impressions of good taste") designed to reveal the condition of the living room and its contents was added. In the third revision the schedule was greatly simplified. Only 17 of the original 53 objective factors were retained; the 4 qualitative elements were retained as in the previous revision. The capacity of an item to differentiate widely separate social classes was the basis of retention. At this time the name was changed to the Social Status Scale 1933.

The new scale attains the ideal of brevity and simplicity. But since it emphasizes material possessions and neglects other classes of objective elements in the home, its general differentiating sensitiveness is probably decidedly less than it would otherwise be. A reliability of 0.96 on a sample of 50 professional men's homes by the test-retest method is reported. Less substantial evidence of merit lies in the author's tests of validity. Correlation ratios of +.57 with occupation and +.44 with income are reported for 442 homes.

Adhering almost entirely to objective elements apparent in family living conditions, McCormick (28) offered a Scale for Measuring Social Adequacy in 1930. A total of 69 separate items are included under the captions: Quality of Neighborhood; Education, Occupation, and Civic Status; Material Status of the Home; and Cultural and Social Influence. This scale covers a greater number of different aspects of family life than any previous one.

With the exception of six graduated items to which arbitrary weights (1, 2, 3, etc.) are given, the questions are reduced to the all-none principle and arbitrary scores of 0–1 assigned. Although the form of the questions would permit the standardized interview technique, it appears from the author's discussion that in the actual collection of the data the schedules were filled in after the interview. A further possibility of unreliability arises from questions pertaining to the delinquency and health history of the members of the family. Because of the self-indictment that information of this kind carries, people are likely to misrepresent the facts. In the original investigation the upper social classes were not asked these questions. An additional point of criticism is the inexactness of judgment arising from questions such as "Are there inartistic prints?" Here individual opinion as to what constitutes an inartistic print is given full sway. This type of question might be diagnostic of aesthetic level, but without the inclusion of a comparative guide it only increases the unreliability of the instrument. Whatever elements of unreliability are contingent on the foregoing are apparently sufficiently compensated for by the length of the scale as well as by the character of the population, since reliability by the method of split halves is 0.96, the highest attained by any of the available measures of home conditions.

The use of an outside criterion against which each item of the scale was validated is the unique feature of the McCormick scale. Defining "social adequacy" as "the quality by which a family maintains a normal life without help from social agencies and institutions," twenty-five judges were asked to rate fourteen groups of families representative of different degrees of social adequacy. The extreme of subadequacy was assigned to "major relief cases involving delinquency," and extreme superadequacy was judged to be found in families of "college graduates of the nonprofessional class with average incomes of over five thousand dollars." Items were regarded as sufficiently diagnostic of social adequacy if they correlated more than $+.30$ or less than $-.30$ with the criterion. Pearson's product-moment coefficient of correlation was used for the quantitative items, and his biserial r for the alternate-response items. Although the lack of evidence of the continuous character of the data and of normal distribution may cause some to question the appropriateness of the biserial r, the method was an economical device for securing the relative significance of items.

The criterion of "social adequacy," however, may be seriously criticized. Dependency alone or in combination with delinquency characterizes the groups classified as inadequate; economic independence is the distinguishing attribute of all the adequate groups. The fact that families are dependent generally makes their delinquencies known. The same delinquencies are not public knowledge in the case of the economically independent and superior families. Further, "adequacy" implies a subjective relationship to individual needs. Certainly the objective factors that comprise the McCormick scale are not diagnostic of "social adequacy." A score earned by this scale would seem rather to represent the relative position of a' particular family with reference to certain environmental factors.

Williams' work (44 and 45) is distinguished for its attempt to measure qualitative aspects of home and neighborhood conditions. He uses the rating scale technique and provides a guide and standard score for the rater's use. Necessities, neatness, size, parental conditions, and parental supervision are considered in the home scale. Regardless of the fact that the scores assigned are purely arbitrary and that statistical analysis is almost wholly lacking, the method is a particularly suggestive approach.

The evaluation of home background by objective tests given to school children was undertaken by Orr (22), working on the Character Education Inquiry of Hartshorne and May (22). On the theory that "manners" might afford a key to refinement of a sort that would be symptomatic of careful family training, Orr constructed an objective test whose scores were in accordance with the judgment of presumably cultivated people. What the Good Manners Test measures is not stated by its author, nor is any statistical analysis offered in defense of its validity or reliability.

Burdick (3), who was also working on the Character Education Inquiry, sought to measure the cultural, economic, and educational level of the home by a method similar to that used by Orr. A correlation of +.50 between the scores of siblings is offered as evidence of reliability. Validity was determined by correlating the children's responses with the Huschka Home Background Scores, as presented by Hartshorne and May (22). This coefficient was +.66. Because of its low reliability and validity the test cannot be considered a satisfactory method of measuring home conditions.

The Huschka Home Background Scores referred to above give numerical values to qualitative descriptions of the home. It represents an earnest attempt to get at qualitative differences in homes, but its general use is distinctly limited.

SUMMARY OF PREVIOUS STUDIES

From our review it appears that the home has been the aspect of the child's environment to which the investigator has turned his attention. Sims and McCormick include two to four items designed to secure an index of the family's participation in community affairs, but in general items reflective of environmental areas other than the home are almost wholly neglected. The two most frequently used single factors indicating the economic and cultural level of the home (occupation and education) are also incorporated in the scales of Sims and McCormick. Neither author reports the respective contributions of these items to the total complex. Chapin omits parental occupation and education entirely. His scale is limited to the material equipment of the living room and its condition.

Unlike persons constructing intelligence tests, most investigators in the field of environment have apparently found the problem of an unselected population an insurmountable one or have failed to recognize its significance in test construction. Chapin's original population, although sampling the entire occupational range, numbered only 38 homes; McCormick had complete records from 184 families, practically all of whom were at one or the other extreme of social position in their community. Sims, however, developed his questionnaire on a relatively large random population of school children (686). No environmental measure standardized from data collected directly in the home and demanding home visitation meets the criterion of an unselected population.

In the construction of instruments to measure environmental status, statistical analysis has been increasing. And although the use of certain statistical techniques may have been inappropriate or even unsound, the increase of quantitative analysis is promising. So far, the criterion of suitability or excellence of any factor or group of factors has been their capacity to differentiate extreme social and economic groups in our society. This is a crude standard. Extremes of any characteristic, human or otherwise, are easily recognizable. Ideally, a scale should be composed of those factors which distinguish the fine gradations existing in our social structure. An economic item should appear in increasing frequency in poor homes, borderline homes, average, better than average, and rich homes. A factor dependent on schooling should progress from the homes of the unschooled to those having the most schooling.

From our review of previous studies it is readily apparent that instruments designed to measure the qualitative aspects of home conditions have been almost entirely neglected. This phase of environment awaits intensive research in the field of the emotions, personality, and attitudes. Until such measures are available, we cannot speak of measuring the relation of home influence to other factors. However adequate our measures of objective factors may be, the question of the effect of antagonism, drive, kindness, etc., on the behavior of children remains unanswered.

PURPOSE OF THE PRESENT STUDY

The purpose of this study is to construct a scale that will give numerical expression to the nature and extent of variation existing in living conditions in urban homes.

In order to approximate the whole complex of conditions under which a family lives, this scale shall include all those aspects of home and community life whose validity can be statistically maintained. For purposes of accuracy in standardization it shall include objective factors only; their existence shall not be a matter of the opinion of the investigator. To insure the highest possible reliability and completeness, all schedules must be filled out in the home by a trained investigator. The population contributing the data for this scale shall be a cross section of American urban families.

II. CONSTRUCTION OF THE SCALE

METHOD OF APPROACH

Since a measure of environment is used primarily in connection with research concerning children and with social service involving the placement of children, it is important to include all those aspects of home and community life that may impinge directly or indirectly on the behavior and development of the child. Hence it was believed desirable to interview at least one child in every home as well as one of the parents. The type and content of the interview was different in the two instances but constant for the two classes of informants. Each was designed to enlist the highest possible degree of cooperation.

EXPERIMENTAL SCHEDULES

In the collection of our data two schedules were used. One, entitled "The Child and His Environment," was designed to record the information gathered from an adult of the household; the other, printed under the same general title but known by its subtitle, "The Interest Interview," was limited to data collected from one of the children in the household. Both were modeled after the form used in the White House Conference study of the preschool child. In constructing the questions we aimed to make them specific and clear. Comparable data was our objective.

An inspection of the schedule "The Child and His Environment" shows that provision is made for two major categories of data. (See the Appendix.) Under "General Information" appear data descriptive of our population — identification, health, and size of family. On the reverse side of this schedule, under the caption "Status Classification," are listed most of the data from which our scale was constructed. Here the questions are classified arbitrarily into groups in order to facilitate the recording of responses and also to permit what seemed in general a coherent interview. As will be seen in Chapters IV and V below, each question is treated independently and then is finally classified according to the opinion of three judges under one of the following headings: Children's Facilities Index, Economic Status Index, Cultural Status Index, Sociality Index, Occupational Status Index, Educational Status Index.

11

The schedule "Interest Interview," on which were recorded the children's responses to 25 questions, included factual and rating questions. (See the Appendix.) As a survey of the questions shows, the purpose of this schedule was to discover the educational and social activities of the child.

In addition to the questions on the printed schedules, seven ratings were made. Four of them were taken directly from Chapin and appear as Part II of his Social Status Scale 1933. They are reproduced herewith:

1. *Cleanliness of room and furnishings*
   a. Spotted or stained.
   b. Dusty.
   c. Spotless and dustless.
2. *Orderliness of room and furnishings*
   a. Articles strewn about in disorder.
   b. Articles in place or in usable order.
3. *Condition of repair of articles and furnishings*
   a. Broken, scratched, frayed, ripped, torn.
   b. Articles or furnishings patched up.
   c. Articles or furnishings in good repair and well kept.
4. *Record your general impression of good taste*
   a. Bizarre, clashing, inharmonious, offensive.
   b. Drab, monotonous, neutral, inoffensive.
   c. Attractive in a positive way, harmonious, quiet, restful.

The other three ratings were as follows:

5. *Exterior of the home*
   1. Very attractive, substantial structure of six rooms or more, costing $10,000 or over.
   2. Average home, costing between $3,000 and $10,000.
   3. Below average structure, costing less than $3,000.
6. *Repair of house*
   1. Building in good repair, house and grounds well kept up. Yes.... No....
7. *Cooperativeness of family*
   1. Indifferent; gave information grudgingly.
   2. Hesitant; after explanation gave information willingly.
   3. Very cooperative.

The presence or absence of three items of household furnishings (desk, table lamps, and fireplace), subsequently thought to be significant but omitted from the original schedule, were written on the margin of the schedule.

In all, 29 questions are listed under "Status Classification." When the independent items grouped under a single question are counted separately, the total is distributed as follows:

Questions demanding yes or no replies............ 66
Quantitative questions......................... 8
Rating questions and classifications.............. 6
                                                 ————
    Total...................................... 80

The grand total of questions analyzed was 84, including those counted above and 4 from the questionnaire given the children.

THE INTERVIEW WITH THE CHILD

Since the purpose of our research was presented to parents as the study of the relation of children's interests to general living conditions, the Interest Interview with the child was usually undertaken first. The procedure was that commonly used in administering the individual mental test. After some general conversation designed to obtain the child's cooperation, the investigator began to question the child. All replies were either recorded by the investigator or checked by the child himself. The form in the Appendix was the schedule used throughout, except that the list of movies (question 10) was changed four times during the two-year period over which the collection of data extended. The need of a current list is obvious. Otherwise memory errors, generally found in questions demanding the recall of past events, would be greatly increased.

Almost without exception the children enjoyed the Interest Interview. It had the appearance of a game. And although it furnished only four questions for our final schedule, "The Minnesota Home Status Index," it provided a point of departure for the interview with the mother. The answers to the questions concerning school studies, collections, wishes, and other matters evoked a prompt response from the mother when they were reported to her.

THE INTERVIEW WITH THE ADULT OF THE HOUSEHOLD

In interviewing the adult of the household, who was almost always the mother, every attempt was made to keep constant the administration of that section of the schedule labeled "Status Classification." Investigators were at liberty to alter the introductory remarks, but ordinarily they were something like this: "Mrs.————, I am going to ask you a number of questions. Many of them may seem unrelated to the child's environment, but since we have no accurate measure of environment, we must include everything that may have any bearing," or, "I am going to ask you many questions. Some will amuse you. All are believed to have some relation to the child's environment."

The recording of the mother's replies followed. Whenever the desired information could be secured by observation, no question was asked. For example, question 15 inquires as to the possession of a number of items, many of which (central heating system, radio, piano) might be visible to the investigator. Where that was the case, the correct reply was circled without further question.

Early in the investigation it was observed that the questions referring to the amount of schooling of parents and to father's occupation (questions 5, 6, and 7) seemed to be embarrassing to some. So instead of asking these questions in the order of their appearance on the schedule, they were held over and asked just previous to question 23, which has to do with the father's membership in clubs, fraternal societies, etc. It was necessary to have the information concerning amount of schooling and occupation at this point in order to determine how many of the items in question 23 had to be asked. A carpenter with sixth-grade schooling would clearly not belong to a scientific society, and the symbol for a negative answer (N) could be encircled without further questioning. Similarly, the investigator could encircle (N) after "trade union" when the father was a surgeon with graduate medical training.

For that part of the experimental schedule classified as "General Information" considerable freedom in presentation was permitted. Questions 1 to 7 were filled out in advance of the personal interview; 11 and 12 were omitted entirely because of the possibility that they would be resented. The name, sex, and age of the child (questions 17, 18, and 19) were known before the home visit was made, though these items were always verified in talking with the mother, generally just after the purpose of the investigation had been explained. Question 26, "Is the family known to any relief agency?" was not asked of the parent. The official records of the Social Service Exchange, with which every family was cleared, provided this information. Answers to questions dealing with the parent's health represented only the informant's judgment in the matter. Inquiry as to the existence of specific disease was not believed pertinent to our main purpose. Questions 23 and 24, concerning the child's health, served as a basis for eliminating those who because of debilitating disease or defect might be denied the opportunities available to normal children in such a family. The writer desired to avoid any selection that might tend to weight the presence or absence of any environmental factor.

III. HOMES PARTICIPATING IN THE STUDY

To secure an adequate sample of the objective differences in urban homes the following criteria were held essential to our investigation: (1) a total population large enough to eliminate the possibility of sampling errors; (2) a population large enough at every socio-economic level to eliminate sampling errors; (3) families of white race only; (4) homes known to have one or more children from 5 to 14 years old.

Six hundred homes were included in the investigation, which represents practically the entire number — all but 2 per cent — invited to participate in the study. In nearly all a personal interview was held with the mother. Only rarely was the father or some other responsible adult our informant. Four hundred children were given the Interest Interview in their homes and the remaining two hundred were interviewed during an individual mental test at the University of Minnesota. As will be seen later in the statistical analysis of our data, the size of the population permitted comparisons in which the disturbing influence of chance was negligible.

Yet one cannot depend on size of population alone to give a representative sample of living conditions. It would be quite possible to select six hundred homes differing only slightly from each other. That such a situation might be avoided, our second criterion was imposed. For our index of socio-economic status, occupation of father was chosen in the belief that this was the best single index available. Consequently a tabulation and classification of parental occupation paralleled the field study in order that a fair sample of homes at each occupational level might be secured.

Our third standard needs little explanation. Living conditions among colored people differ so greatly from those among whites that it did not seem possible to construct a scale applicable to both races.

Limiting the homes to those having children from 5 to 14 years of age (our fourth criterion) served two purposes. First, it provided a population similar in composition to that for which the final scale would be most useful — namely, elementary school children, who are more frequently the subjects of research than any other single group of children. Secondly, it eliminated families that had only begun the operation of a home and hence had accumulated little and included families that had existed long enough to have attained their stride in the social complex of the community.

RESOURCES

The task of selecting families to fit our criteria demanded careful planning if any efficiency was to be attained in our investigation. Once a family with children of the desired ages had been located, the father's occupation was checked — the current issue of the city directory serving as a preliminary guide. If the father's occupation had shifted downward since the depression of 1929, the work pursued previous to 1929 was regarded as his typical or modal occupation. This was the situation in the case of several men in the building trades and manufacturing industry. The Nursery School files and those of the Parent Education Department of the Institute of Child Welfare at the University of Minnesota supplied the largest number of subjects. They provided about 275 cases located in Minneapolis and St. Paul. About 190 families of adopted children, residing in Minneapolis, St. Paul, Duluth, Rochester, Faribault, and Owatonna, Minnesota, were furnished by a study in progress under the direction of the writer. Two Minneapolis settlement houses, namely, North East Neighborhood House and Pillsbury House, provided 100 and 35 families, respectively. Their files, like those of the Institute, were carefully checked for age of child and parental occupation. Fifteen families were supplied by the Prescott Public School in Minneapolis.

DESCRIPTION OF GROUP SELECTED

If the Minnesota Home Status Index is subsequently demonstrated to have any merit as a measuring instrument of family living conditions, it will be due in no small part to the character of the population on which it was constructed. Table 1 shows the number and percentage frequency at each occupational level. One would prefer, of course, that the occupational distribution of the group be exactly the same as that of the general population, but the attainment of this ideal was impossible. However, as is apparent in Table 1 and the map below (Figure 1), the number of cases at each occupational level is large enough to prevent sampling errors. Further, it was possible to draw standard samples from the total group in which the distribution of the male occupation was the same as in the general population. Of additional significance is the fact that the total number provided a large population on which to validate individual items.

The average size of family corresponds to that in the general population. According to estimates made from the United States census of 1930, about 3.3 is the average number of children per family in Minnesota. This figure is based on both rural and urban populations. Our experimental group averaged 3.0 children per

TABLE 1. — OCCUPATIONAL DISTRIBUTION OF THE EXPERIMENTAL GROUP

Occupational Classification *	Number	Percentage	Percentage in the General Male Population, 1930†
I. Professional	94	15.8	4.2
II. Semiprofessional and managerial	97	16.3	9.6
III. Skilled trades, clerical	135	22.7	22.0
IV. Farmers	0	0.0	0.0
V. Semiskilled occupations, minor clerical, and minor business	150	25.2	42.6
VI. Slightly skilled trades, occupations requiring little training	68	11.4	8.2
VII. Day laborers of all classes	51	8.6	13.4

* F. L. Goodenough and J. E. Anderson, *Experimental Child Study* (Century Co., New York, 1931), pp. 237, 501 ff.

† H. J. Green *et al*, *A Manual of Selected Occupational Tests for Use in Public Employment Offices* (Employment Stabilization Research Institute Bulletins, Vol. 2, No. 3, University of Minnesota Press, July, 1933).

family. The fact that our families are residents of urban communities, where in general families are smaller, may explain the lower average. Or it may be due in part to the inclusion of households having adopted children. A single adopted child is the rule rather than the exception. Thus the number of one-child families would be increased and our average size of family decreased. However, the difference between the general population and our experimental group is slight.

Since the age of the children probably affects the accumulation of certain cultural materials in a family and determines the community connections of the parents, the character of our experimental group in respect to age should be noted. The average age of the children is 9.9 years; standard deviation, 2.6. If all were "only" or "oldest" children, then we might assume that the age of our homes corresponded to that of the children. A preponderance of "only" and "oldest" over "youngest" and "middle" sibling positions at any

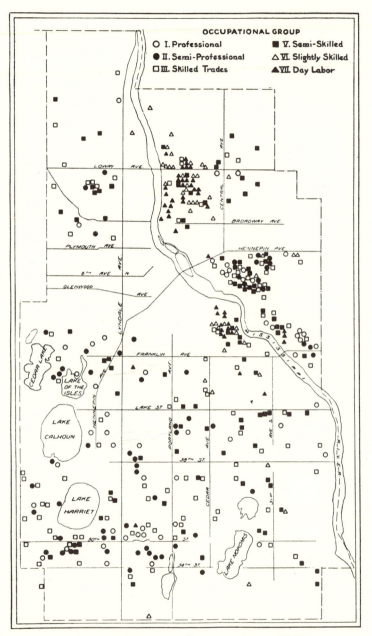

Figure 1. — Location According to Occupation of the 400 Minneapolis Homes Included in This Study

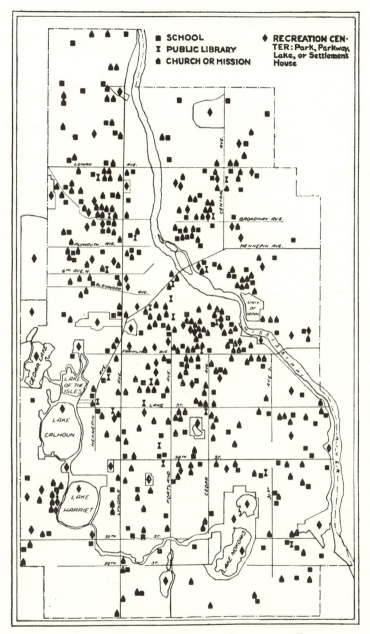

■ SCHOOL
X PUBLIC LIBRARY
▲ CHURCH OR MISSION
♦ RECREATION CEN-
TER: Park, Parkway,
Lake, or Settlement
House

FIGURE 2. — LOCATION OF EDUCATIONAL AND RECREATIONAL FACILITIES
IN MINNEAPOLIS, 1934

19

age level would conceivably affect our population. The greatest limitation to a fair sample of the general school population, however, would occur in the instance of our 5- and 6-year-olds, since their homes would fall below one standard deviation of the age of the entire group. An analysis of our 5- and 6-year-old children showed an almost perfect balance between "only" and "oldest" on the one hand and "youngest" and "middle" sibling positions on the other. In the first group we have 36 children and in the latter 34. Our population therefore includes only 36 homes that are as young as 6 or 7 years, assuming that the home was established from one to two years before the birth of the child. A similar analysis at each age level is probably desirable, but since a study of the mean scores of each age group and an analysis of the separate items believed to be contingent on age showed no significant difference, sibling position was not considered further.

An additional factor that might materially distort certain elements in family living conditions is the fact of a broken home. In 2.5 per cent of the cases only one of the parents was in the home. This figure is somewhat lower than that for the general population if divorce rates are taken as the index of broken homes. If homes broken by the death of one parent are included in the comparison, our population is obviously not typical of the general population. It represents homes where the environmental factors are little affected by the element of a broken home.

The similarity of our experimental population to other adult populations is indicated in the correlations shown in Table 2. The

TABLE 2. — CORRELATION OF FATHER'S OCCUPATION WITH OTHER FACTORS

Correlated Factor	Number of Cases	Product Moment Correlation
Father's Otis mental test score	291	.60
Father's mental age	291	.60
Father's Stanford-Binet vocabulary	284	.60
Mother's Otis mental test score	310	.49
Mother's mental age	310	.48
Mother's Stanford-Binet vocabulary	308	.48

magnitude of these correlations corresponds with those found by Jones (31) and other investigators.

The accessibility of public institutions (schools, churches, libraries, recreation centers) to all of our homes may be seen from the map on page 19. The district north of Broadway and east of the

river, in which almost all of the fathers are in the two lowest occupational groups, has nearly as many institutions as the area
south of Lake Street and west of Portland, where the fathers are
in the two highest occupational groups. The neighborhood between
Franklin and the river abounds in facilities for education and culture. Incidentally, these maps show that proximity to cultural centers, as a measure of environment, lacks power to differentiate.
Seemingly, cultural centers are widely distributed in modern urban
communities.

IV. DISCUSSION OF FINDINGS

Since, as has been previously stated, this investigation is a study of the objective elements of the child's environment as material for direct analysis, our problem is, first, the selection of factors that differentiate family living conditions; second, the determination of the differentiating power of these factors; and third, the incorporation of the most discriminating factors into a scale that may be readily and efficiently administered.

NUMBER AND RANGE OF FACTORS STUDIED

On the theory that the value of our scale would depend on the adequacy with which it samples the entire content of family living conditions, all published scales were reviewed. About 32 items were selected from them. To these, 52 others were arbitrarily added, making a total of 84 items. Other things being equal, the greater the number of items in a scale the greater will be its discriminative value so far as the whole of family living conditions is concerned.

The next consideration was the range of family life covered by the items. As has been pointed out by other investigators, a scale with high differentiating power may be of little value for use with small populations because it exercises its power over a narrow field. Take, for example, scales based on the single factor of occupation, or education, or income. Homes may be similar in any one of these respects and yet be very different from each other. Conversely, they may be dissimilar in some respects and still be similar in many others. Of the currently used scales, Chapin's asks a number of questions about one aspect of home equipment — the living room. An inspection of our list of items (Table 3) shows that many aspects of family life are covered: the entire household equipment, the cultural facilities of the home, the educational level of the parents, the occupation of the father, extra-school opportunities for the children, participation of the parents in community activities, and the character of the neighborhood.

GENERAL RESPONSE

Before dealing with the second aspect of our problem, the determination of the differentiating power of the factors, the general response to our inquiry was tabulated. (See Table 3.)

The first part of Table 3 lists the replies to the 70 alternative-response (yes-no) questions of our schedule. The replies to the 8 graduated and the 6 rating items follow.

An analysis of the alternative-response items shows that 86 per cent of them were answered by 90 to 100 per cent of the population. Reliable information as to relief and delinquency (items 2, 3, and 4) was available only for Minneapolis and St. Paul residents because social service clearings, the only dependable source for such data, do not exist in the smaller cities. Question 32, relative to ownership of a country or lake home, was not added until the study was well under way, hence the small percentage of replies. The graduated and rating items were present to some degree in 100 per cent of the cases.

POSSESSION OF SPECIFIED ITEMS

The percentage of the population possessing the individual items varies from item to item, as may be seen in Table 3. Apparently some items are relatively common — for example, number 10, a central heating system; 12, a vacuum cleaner; and 15, a radio. Others appear only rarely. A consideration of frequency of occurrence or possession will enter into our subsequent discussion of the score value of the items.

DIFFERENTIATING POWER OF FACTORS

In the absence of an outside criterion, two methods are available for determining the differentiating power of the items composing a scale: (1) the determination of the correlation of each item with the total of all others and (2) the comparison of the frequency of occurrence of each item in relationship to total score in selected segments of the distribution. Both methods are dependent on total score, and both assume that total score is an adequate criterion for validation. Further, both assume that the items are distributed normally in the general population.

The application of the first method to our data would involve for each item the calculation of the biserial r between the group possessing the item and the group not possessing it. It would necessitate the computation of as many scores for each home included in the study as there are items in our schedule. This method was used by Sims (34). Taking +.44 as the discriminating coefficient, he included in his final scale all items that correlated +.44 or higher with the remaining average score of those homes possessing and those

Environmental Item	Number Answering Question	Percentage of Total		
		Answering Question	Not Possessing Item	Possessing Item
1. Mother not employed	571	95.4	10.7	89.3
2. No relief before 1929	344	57.5	19.2	80.8
3. No relief after 1929	345	57.7	25.5	74.5
4. No juvenile court delinquency record	344	57.5	13.1	86.9
5. No stores in block	598	99.7	81.8	18.2
6. Home not connected with store	596	99.3	2.5	97.5
7. No factories within 3 blocks	597	99.5	27.0	73.0
8. Parents not separated or divorced	589	98.2	3.6	96.4
9. Do not rent home	583	97.2	37.9	62.1
10. Central heating system	600	100.0	21.8	78.2
11. Telephone	600	100.0	33.3	66.7
12. Vacuum cleaner	600	100.0	22.8	77.2
13. Automobile	600	100.0	29.8	70.2
14. Second automobile	600	100.0	92.3	7.7
15. Radio	597	99.5	13.6	86.4
16. Piano	600	100.0	39.0	61.0
17. Second bathroom	600	100.0	89.2	10.8
18. Washing machine and mangle	600	100.0	71.2	28.8
19. Electric refrigerator	600	100.0	74.0	26.0
20. Folding camera	600	100.0	50.3	49.7
21. Moving picture camera	600	100.0	94.3	5.7
22. Playground equipment	600	100.0	65.7	34.3
23. Nursery or recreational room	599	99.8	81.3	18.7
24. Boat	599	99.8	87.3	12.7
25. Bicycle or tricycle	600	100.0	50.3	49.7
26. Typewriter	600	100.0	72.5	27.5
27. Fireplace	584	97.3	65.8	34.2
28. Ventilating fan for kitchen	584	97.3	69.3	30.7
29. Desk	584	97.3	69.3	30.7
30. Table lamps	580	96.7	54.8	45.2
31. Metropolitan newspaper other than local	591	98.5	94.2	5.8
32. Country or lake home	214	35.9	90.7	9.3
33. Vacations for family members	596	99.3	36.6	63.4
34. Either parent plays musical instrument	598	99.7	43.8	56.2
35. House in good repair	424	70.8	18.2	81.8
36. Paid assistance in home	591	98.5	73.3	26.7
37. Two or more daily newspapers	595	99.2	80.4	19.6
38. Encyclopedia	595	99.2	48.4	51.6
39. Preventive dental treatment for child	588	97.8	22.6	77.4
Father's Membership in:				
40. Professional or scientific society	586	97.7	79.0	21.0
41. Civic club	586	97.7	75.8	24.2
42. Trade union	587	97.8	84.2	15.8
43. Parent-teachers association	587	97.8	61.7	38.3
44. Study club	587	97.8	90.5	9.5
45. Fraternal organization	587	97.8	47.7	52.3

TABLE 3. — *Continued*

Environmental Item	Number Answering Question	Percentage of Total		
		Answering Question	Not Possessing Item	Possessing Item
46. Social club	586	97.7	65.4	34.6
47. University extension course	587	97.8	92.3	7.7
Mother's Membership in:				
48. Professional or scientific society	592	98.7	95.1	4.9
49. Civic club	592	98.7	86.0	14.0
50. Parent-teachers association	592	98.7	36.8	63.2
51. Study club	592	98.7	68.9	31.1
52. Fraternal organization	592	98.7	69.4	30.6
53. Social club	592	98.7	54.1	45.9
54. University extension course	592	98.7	94.8	5.2
Either Parent's Participation in:				
55. Fishing or hunting	596	99.3	32.4	67.6
56. Bridge	596	99.3	46.0	54.0
57. Tennis or golf	596	99.3	69.1	30.9
58. Horseback riding	595	99.2	94.5	5.5
Private Instruction for Child in:				
59. Music	586	97.7	61.5	38.4
60. Dancing	586	97.7	80.2	19.8
61. Art	586	97.7	98.6	1.4
62. Expression or dramatics	586	97.7	91.8	8.2
63. Foreign language	586	97.7	98.3	1.7
Children:				
64. In camps:				
Charity	536	89.4	92.4	7.6
Subsidized	536	89.4	90.7	9.3
Exclusive	536	89.4	96.6	3.4
65. In pay clubs	534	89.0	64.6	35.4
66. In leadership positions	537	89.5	49.2	50.8
67. Attend Sunday School	540	90.0	27.4	72.6
68. Attend movies twice a month or oftener	543	90.5	64.6	35.4
69. Have public or school bank account	540	90.0	40.6	59.4
70. Have regular allowance	539	89.9	72.4	27.6
71. Collections made by children	548	91.4	56.9	43.1
72. Education of father	559	93.2	00.0	100.0
73. Education of mother	571	95.2	00.0	100.0
74. Occupational classification of father	595	99.2	00.0	100.0
75. Room-person ratio	596	99.3	00.0	100.0
76. Number of children's books	596	99.3	00.0	100.0
77. Number of other books	591	98.5	00.0	100.0
78. Number of magazines	600	100.0	00.0	100.0
79. Cultural content score of magazines	599	99.8	00.0	100.0
80. Structure of house	598	99.7	00.0	100.0
81. Cleanliness	425	70.8	00.0	100.0
82. Orderliness	423	70.5	00.0	100.0
83. Good taste	420	70.0	00.0	100.0
84. Condition of furnishings	424	70.7	00.0	100.0

not possessing the item. The assumption underlying this method is that items that correlate high with the remaining items for possession and nonpossession are measures of a common variable.

The second method, known as the criterion of internal consistency, also presumes to select the items measuring a single common variable and, as previously stated, assumes that total score is an adequate index for validation. It was chosen for this study because its determination is less laborious than the first method. Although it is not a new technique, having long been used by persons constructing objective tests to evaluate the differentiating power of separate test questions, this is the first time that it has been applied to data of this type.

As usually applied, the criterion of internal consistency is the ability of an item to differentiate between extremes of the distribution of total scores. In these data its purpose would be to discover the extent to which each item distinguishes between rich and poor or high- and low-income homes — richness and poorness being determined by the total score that a home makes on the scale as a whole. Previous investigators have used various proportions of cases at the extremes in making their analyses. Obviously, the smaller the proportion the more likely it is that the frequency of possession in the segments will differ. In this field of research, as in others, extreme distinctions are readily made.

Since our data number 600, it was believed desirable to use a proportion that would provide subgroups large enough to prevent the sampling errors that are inevitable in a small population, yet small enough to get a clear demarcation of the frequency of possession of the items. Twenty per cent was arbitrarily chosen. This figure yielded 120 cases at each extreme, and, as will be shown later, the contrast between these two groups was significantly different for every item.

From the first acceptance of the test of internal consistency as our validating criterion it was decided to extend the standard to the cases located between the extremes. Clearly a more discriminating aggregate of items would thus be assembled. Certainly an item capable of making fine distinctions throughout the entire distribution is superior to one that differentiates only the extremes. Our standard, arbitrarily defined, classified an item as discriminating if, besides differentiating the extreme fifths or quintile groups of the distribution, it also differentiated two of the other four successive quintile groups.

PROCEDURE IN VALIDATION OF ITEMS

The procedure used in determining the validity of our individual items is as follows:

1. Every schedule was marked for total score by crediting the presence or possession of each item. In the case of graduated items, "presence" was taken at any point beyond the 50th percentile of the entire group. For example, the 50th percentile in the case of the number of magazines received in the homes lies between 3 and 4; consequently those homes taking 4 or more magazines were credited as possessing that item. To receive credit for having children's books the home must have had at least 11. For school grade attainment, the 50th percentile for the mothers fell between the ninth and tenth grade; for the fathers between the tenth and eleventh. Consequently only those mothers who had gone as far as the tenth grade or beyond, and only those fathers who had gone at least as far as the eleventh grade received credit for the possession of formal education. When weights were determined in computing final scores, each graduated level was assigned a numerical value.

2. The schedules were next arranged according to total score and then divided into fifths. The 600 schedules were thus grouped into packs of 120 each, the top fifth, or quintile, constituting the 120 homes receiving the highest scores, the fourth quintile those securing the next highest scores, and so on down to the 120 homes receiving the lowest total scores, which constitute the first quintile.

3. At this point the presence of the item in each of the groups was tallied. Thus if an item appeared in 90 of the 120 homes in the highest group, in 60 of the 120 homes in the next highest, in 40 in the next, 30 in the next, and finally in 15 homes in the lowest total score group, the percentage frequency of possession in the successive quintiles would be 75, 50, 33, 25, and 13 per cent, respectively.

In Table 4 is shown the percentage frequency of occurrence in successive fifths of the entire population. From this table one can see that in general the percentage frequency of occurrence of an item progresses from quintile 1 to quintile 5. In some instances the difference between successive quintiles is strikingly large, as in the case of "playground equipment." In others only 3 of the 5 quintile levels differ markedly in the percentage of possession. Take, for example, the item "telephone." Only a slight difference between the two highest total score groups (quintiles 4 and 5) is evident, whereas the magnitude of the difference between the other three groups is noticeably large.

Environmental Item	Quin-tile 1 Per Cent	Quin-tile 2 Per Cent	Quin-tile 3 Per Cent	Quin-tile 4 Per Cent	Quin-tile 5 Per Cent
1. Mother not employed	81.4	86.8	89.6	94.7	93.7
2. No relief before 1929	47.6	79.1	93.2	98.3	97.3
3. No relief after 1929	32.1	68.7	88.1	96.1	100.0
4. No juvenile court delinquency record	64.3	83.6	98.3	94.9	100.0
5. No stores in block	56.8	66.7	83.3	93.3	94.2
6. Home not connected with store	94.9	95.8	97.5	100.0	99.2
7. No factories within 3 blocks	32.2	60.5	81.5	92.5	96.7
8. Parents not separated or divorced	92.1	95.8	100.0	99.2	99.2
9. Do not rent home	35.9	54.5	68.6	70.3	81.2
10. Central heating system	27.5	76.7	92.5	96.7	99.2
11. Telephone	8.3	51.7	79.2	94.2	96.7
12. Vacuum cleaner	17.5	75.0	95.0	99.2	98.3
13. Automobile	22.5	59.2	79.2	92.5	96.7
14. Second automobile	0.8	1.7	3.3	5.0	30.0
15. Radio	48.3	94.2	95.0	97.5	98.3
16. Piano	16.7	50.0	66.7	84.2	85.0
17. Second bathroom	0.8	7.5	5.0	11.7	29.2
18. Washing machine and mangle	13.3	15.8	20.8	40.8	54.2
19. Electric refrigerator	0.8	5.0	19.2	40.8	64.2
20. Folding camera	12.5	28.3	54.2	68.3	85.0
21. Moving picture camera	0.0	0.8	0.8	5.0	21.7
22. Playground equipment	4.2	15.8	30.8	46.7	74.2
23. Nursery or recreational room	0.8	5.0	15.0	23.3	50.0
24. Boat	0.8	7.5	14.2	15.0	26.7
25. Bicycle or tricycle	18.3	35.8	49.2	62.5	81.7
26. Typewriter	3.3	13.3	30.8	43.3	47.5
27. Fireplace	5.9	11.3	30.8	40.7	82.6
28. Ventilating fan for kitchen	0.0	0.8	1.7	5.0	10.0
29. Desk	4.2	20.9	29.9	43.6	48.3
30. Table lamps	31.1	45.5	43.1	44.9	58.6
31. Metropolitan newspaper other than local	0.0	2.6	3.4	9.3	13.6
32. Country or lake home	0.0	0.0	14.7	18.7	50.0
33. Vacations for family members	24.6	50.0	68.1	81.5	92.5
34. Either parent plays musical instrument	28.6	37.5	55.0	77.3	80.0
35. House in good repair	41.1	82.1	92.1	96.3	100.0
36. Paid assistance in home	2.6	7.6	8.3	42.7	72.3
37. Two or more daily newspapers	1.7	22.0	30.0	44.6	63.0
38. Encyclopedia	8.2	33.9	61.7	72.1	82.1
39. Preventive dental treatment for child	26.3	51.7	64.6	85.7	93.2
Father's Membership in:					
40. Professional or scientific society	0.0	0.9	12.1	30.0	59.2
41. Civic club	2.6	10.3	19.8	30.8	55.8
42. Trade union	0.0	0.9	2.0	0.0	2.6
43. Parent-teachers association	8.8	22.4	33.3	56.7	70.0
44. Study club	0.9	1.7	2.6	14.2	28.3
45. Fraternal organization	26.3	42.2	48.7	66.7	77.5
46. Social club	2.6	17.2	31.6	47.5	73.3
47. University extension course	0.0	0.9	9.4	7.5	20.0
Mother's Membership in:					
48. Professional or scientific society	0.0	0.0	5.0	3.4	15.4
49. Civic club	0.9	6.8	6.7	21.8	35.9

28

TABLE 4. — *Continued*

Environmental Item	Quin-tile 1 Per Cent	Quin-tile 2 Per Cent	Quin-tile 3 Per Cent	Quin-tile 4 Per Cent	Quin-tile 5 Per Cent
50. Parent-teachers association	19.0	53.0	69.2	80.7	94.0
51. Study club	3.4	11.1	25.8	46.2	69.2
52. Fraternal organization	16.4	24.8	26.7	38.7	46.2
53. Social club	9.5	35.0	48.3	58.0	79.5
54. University extension course	0.0	0.8	5.0	5.9	14.5
Either Parent's Participation in:					
55. Fishing or hunting	37.3	65.5	81.7	74.2	81.5
56. Bridge	5.9	31.9	62.5	83.3	87.4
57. Tennis or golf	1.7	6.7	23.3	47.5	74.8
58. Horseback riding	0.0	0.8	5.8	8.4	12.6
Private Instruction for Child in:					
59. Music	4.2	20.2	47.5	54.2	64.1
60. Dancing	1.7	9.6	23.7	25.8	38.5
61. Art	0.0	0.0	0.8	1.7	0.4
62. Expression or dramatics	0.0	0.9	11.0	11.7	17.1
63. Foreign language	0.0	0.0	0.8	1.7	6.0
Children:					
64. In camps:					
Charity	28.7	7.2	0.9	0.0	0.0
Subsidized	1.8	2.1	11.9	11.5	16.8
Exclusive	0.0	1.0	1.0	3.5	8.0
65. In pay clubs	17.0	27.3	42.9	42.9	48.2
66. In leadership positions	31.1	47.5	62.4	59.8	55.9
67. Attend Sunday School	68.9	72.0	77.3	75.2	67.5
68. Attend movies twice a month or oftener	34.9	45.0	28.8	29.5	41.2
69. Have public or school bank account	13.8	43.4	58.2	69.4	76.8
70. Have regular allowance	10.3	12.9	20.7	40.5	51.8
71. Collections made by children	28.4	44.6	46.8	49.6	43.9
72. Education of father:					
Some grade school	90.1	61.9	33.6	21.2	10.1
Some high school	7.0	17.1	21.5	14.3	5.0
Completed high school	2.0	13.3	24.1	17.0	12.6
Some college	0.0	2.0	8.6	17.7	11.7
Completed college	1.0	4.8	9.5	19.5	31.1
Graduate work	0.0	1.0	2.6	10.2	29.5
73. Education of mother:					
Some grade school	80.2	59.8	37.1	18.8	8.3
Some high school	12.3	20.6	22.5	16.2	15.9
Completed high school	7.6	13.4	22.4	33.3	26.7
Some college	0.0	3.6	13.8	17.9	23.3
Completed college	0.0	1.8	3.4	12.8	24.2
Graduate work	0.0	0.9	0.9	0.9	1.6
74. Occupational classification of father:					
VII. Day labor	34.7	8.5	0.0	0.0	0.0
VI. Slightly skilled	32.2	18.8	3.3	3.3	0.0
V. Semiskilled	21.2	46.2	37.5	20.0	1.7
IV. Farmer	...	...	...	...	...
III. Skilled trades and clerical	11.9	20.5	39.2	25.0	16.7
II. Semiprofessional and managerial	0.0	4.3	12.5	30.9	33.3
I. Profession	0.0	1.7	7.5	20.8	48.3

TABLE 4. — *Continued*

Environmental Item	Quin-tile 1 Per Cent	Quin-tile 2 Per Cent	Quin-tile 3 Per Cent	Quin-tile 4 Per Cent	Quin-tile 5 Per Cent
75. Room-person ratio:					
0.25–1.49	89.2	67.2	42.0	32.2	36.7
1.50–1.74	3.3	15.1	29.4	28.8	25.8
1.75–1.99	0.8	2.5	1.7	8.5	12.5
2.00–2.24	3.3	13.4	22.7	24.6	13.3
2.25 and over	3.3	1.6	4.2	5.9	11.6
76. Number of children's books:					
1–10	88.2	55.5	25.2	10.9	2.5
11–30	10.1	31.1	47.1	32.8	17.5
31–50	1.7	7.6	13.4	21.8	23.3
Over 50	0.0	5.9	14.3	34.4	56.7
77. Number of other books in home library:					
1–50	97.4	79.8	50.4	30.5	13.3
51–100	1.7	10.9	24.8	17.8	10.8
101–250	0.8	6.7	18.0	29.7	35.8
251–500	0.0	1.7	4.3	15.2	20.0
Over 500	0.0	0.8	2.6	6.8	20.0
78. Number of magazines:					
1–3	98.3	80.0	45.8	22.5	6.7
4	1.7	9.2	19.2	20.8	10.8
5	0.0	6.7	15.0	15.8	11.7
6 and over	0.0	4.2	20.0	40.8	70.8
79. Cultural content score of magazines:					
0– 9.9	89.0	61.7	30.0	12.5	4.2
10–19.9	10.1	31.7	31.7	30.9	10.0
20–29.9	0.0	4.2	31.7	37.5	31.7
30–39.9	0.8	1.7	5.8	10.8	35.8
40–49.9	0.0	0.8	0.0	5.9	10.8
50–59.9	0.0	0.0	0.8	2.5	6.6
60–69.9	0.0	0.0	0.0	0.0	0.8

At this point one might proceed to select the items, declaring items to be valid measures of environmental differences if the percentage difference between the extreme quintiles and successive quintiles met a certain minimum standard. Such an arbitrary procedure would not work serious harm so far as our data go. However, our interest is in the predictive value of the items, i.e., in the probability of the occurrence of a similar difference in another sampling of homes. The fact, for example, that a difference of 5 per cent or more is maintained between successive quintiles for "electric refrigerator" tells us nothing as to the stability of this difference. Would further samples of homes give approximately the same difference? Or is it probable that the difference would be reduced to zero, or even reversed?

4. To test the stability of the observed differences between suc-

cessive quintiles before deciding on the discriminating value of the items, we proceeded to determine the probability of the occurrence of a difference greater than zero between two percentages. The first step in our procedure here was the calculation of the standard error of a proportion for which the Edgerton-Paterson Table of Standard Errors and Percentages (15) was used. Then the formula for determining the standard error of a difference between two proportions, i.e., σ diff. $= \sqrt{\sigma_1{}^2 + \sigma_2{}^2}$, was applied. Assuming that the distribution of differences in an infinite number of samples would follow a normal curve with the obtained differences as the most probable mean difference, our next step was the determination of the ratio of each obtained difference to its standard error. This told us, in sigma units, how far a zero difference is below its mean. The translation into "chances" of occurrence for other, similarly chosen, populations was read from the Kelley-Wood Table of Normal Probability Integral (25). Since minus 3 sigma includes practically all the cases in the distribution of differences below the mean, it is usually customary to regard a $\dfrac{D}{\sigma \text{ diff.}}$ of 3 as indicative of complete reliability, i.e., 1,000 chances in 1,000 for the recurrence of the observed phenomenon. When $\dfrac{D}{\sigma \text{ diff.}}$ is zero, the chances of occurrence and non-occurrence are even, i.e., the chances are said to be fifty-fifty.

The analysis according to the foregoing method is presented in Table 5. Note should be made that the table includes not only the statistics for estimating the probability of occurrence of a similar difference between successive quintiles, but also the probability of occurrence of a similar difference between the two extreme quintiles, the highest total score group (quintile 5) and the lowest total score group (quintile 1).

An inspection of Table 5 shows that, taking all the items together, the chances are practically 1,000 in 1,000 that in another sampling of homes differences between quintile 1 and quintile 5 would be in the same direction. Successive quintiles (1 and 2, 2 and 3, 3 and 4, and 4 and 5) are similarly differentiated for several of the items — for example, folding camera, playground equipment, and vacations. The difference for some of the other items, i.e., second automobile, home not connected with a store, and mother not employed, are not great. Some items, the electric refrigerator, for example, fail to differentiate the two lowest quintiles while clearly discriminating between the others. The reverse is true of the tele-

TABLE 5. — PROBABILITY OF THE RECURRENCE OF A DIFFERENCE SIMILAR TO THE
OBSERVED ONE BETWEEN SUCCESSIVE QUINTILES AND EXTREME QUINTILES OF
THE ENTIRE POPULATION IN ANOTHER SAMPLING OF HOMES

(Expressed by the critical ratio $\dfrac{D}{\sigma\,\text{diff.}}$.)

Environmental Item	Quin-tiles 1 and 2	Quin-tiles 2 and 3	Quin-tiles 3 and 4	Quin-tiles 4 and 5	Quin-tiles 1 and 5
1. Mother not employed	1.10	0.65	1.44	0.26	2.87
2. No relief before 1929	4.24	2.35	1.34	0.36	8.48
3. No relief after 1929	4.77	2.72	1.76	1.50	13.24
4. No juvenile court delinquency record	2.76	3.02	0.99	1.78	6.66
5. No stores in block	1.56	3.01	2.44	0.28	7.33
6. Home not connected with store	0.33	0.68	1.85	0.08	1.50
7. No factories within 3 blocks	4.51	3.64	2.52	1.40	13.96
8. Parents not separated or divorced	1.17	2.28	0.83	0.00	2.57
9. Do not rent home	2.85	2.20	0.28	1.94	7.82
10. Central heating system	8.72	3.42	1.41	1.34	17.03
11. Telephone	8.28	4.63	3.44	0.92	29.66
12. Vacuum cleaner	10.75	4.45	1.86	0.55	21.32
13. Automobile	6.19	3.40	2.94	1.41	17.87
14. Second automobile	0.55	0.77	0.64	5.34	6.77
15. Radio	9.00	0.27	1.03	0.43	10.46
16. Piano	5.78	2.65	3.18	0.17	14.29
17. Second bathroom	2.48	0.77	3.21	3.40	6.45
18. Washing machine and mangle	0.54	0.99	3.40	2.08	7.41
19. Electric refrigerator	1.86	3.41	3.72	3.73	14.03
20. Folding camera	3.09	4.20	2.24	3.08	16.26
21. Moving picture camera	0.83	0.00	1.86	3.85	5.68
22. Playground equipment	3.02	2.76	2.54	4.49	15.76
23. Nursery or recreational room	1.86	2.58	1.64	4.46	10.47
24. Boat	2.48	1.64	0.17	2.22	6.15
25. Bicycle or tricycle	3.09	2.10	2.07	3.36	12.63
26. Typewriter	2.86	3.31	2.00	0.64	9.08
27. Fireplace	1.60	3.76	1.59	7.34	20.08
28. Ventilating fan for kitchen	0.10	0.61	1.22	1.44	3.57
29. Desk	3.93	1.57	2.17	0.71	8.78
30. Table lamps	0.69	0.36	0.28	2.10	4.38
31. Metropolitan newspaper other than local	1.60	0.40	1.17	1.00	4.18
32. Country or lake home	0.00	2.41	0.44	0.87	1.41
33. Vacations for family members	4.16	2.87	2.36	2.52	14.32
34. Either parent plays musical instrument	1.46	2.77	3.70	0.50	9.24
35. House in good repair	6.11	1.90	1.09	1.67	11.28
36. Paid assistance in home	1.66	0.20	6.54	4.76	15.59
37. Two or more daily newspapers	3.92	2.13	1.84	1.55	9.77
38. Encyclopedia	5.07	4.44	1.70	1.82	16.91
39. Preventive dental treatment for child	4.10	2.01	3.83	1.87	13.97
Father's Membership in:					
40. Professional or scientific society	0.92	3.49	3.43	4.72	13.07
41. Civic club	2.35	2.02	1.93	3.99	10.92
42. Trade union	4.06	1.87	1.32	1.06	0.13
43. Parent-teachers association	2.88	1.86	3.70	2.13	12.19
44. Study club	0.48	0.43	3.23	2.68	6.41
45. Fraternal organization	2.56	0.99	2.83	1.87	9.06
46. Social club	3.87	2.58	2.51	4.19	16.40
47. University extension course	0.92	2.97	0.53	2.86	5.40

TABLE 5. — *Continued*

Environmental Item	Quin-tiles 1 and 2	Quin-tiles 2 and 3	Quin-tiles 3 and 4	Quin-tiles 4 and 5	Quin-tiles 1 and 5
Mother's Membership in:					
48. Professional or scientific society	0.00	2.46	0.61	3.17	4.50
49. Civic club	2.28	0.03	3.35	2.36	7.64
50. Parent-teachers association	5.67	2.54	2.05	3.11	17.40
51. Study club	2.29	2.94	3.76	3.64	14.27
52. Fraternal organization	1.58	0.33	3.65	1.16	5.16
53. Social club	6.63	2.08	1.50	3.64	14.89
54. University extension course	0.82	1.86	0.30	2.17	4.48
Either Parent's Participation in:					
55. Fishing or hunting	4.50	2.87	1.39	1.35	7.73
56. Bridge	5.35	4.93	3.68	0.88	21.22
57. Tennis or golf	0.18	3.61	4.00	4.48	17.28
58. Horseback riding	0.83	2.07	0.78	1.05	4.04
Private Instruction for Child in:					
59. Music	3.52	4.56	1.04	1.57	11.74
60. Dancing	2.49	2.88	0.37	2.10	7.81
61. Art	0.00	0.10	0.61	0.00	0.00
62. Expression or dramatics	0.09	3.28	0.17	1.18	5.00
63. Foreign language	0.00	0.10	0.61	1.53	2.67
Children:					
64. In camps:					
Charity	4.19	2.19	0.83	0.00	6.52
Subsidized	0.15	2.73	0.09	1.12	3.97
Exclusive	0.94	0.00	1.28	1.47	3.08
65. In pay clubs	1.78	2.35	0.00	0.79	5.23
66. In leadership positions	2.42	2.18	0.40	0.59	3.76
67. Attend Sunday School	0.48	0.87	0.36	1.27	0.23
68. Attend movies twice a month or oftener	1.47	2.44	0.95	1.86	0.96
69. Have public or school bank account	4.92	2.14	1.72	1.23	12.07
70. Have regular allowance	0.58	1.51	3.24	1.69	7.42
71. Collections made by children	2.44	0.32	0.42	0.86	2.43
72. Education of father:					
Some high school	2.33	1.23	0.63	2.43	0.61
Completed high school	3.11	2.08	1.33	0.94	3.08
Some college	1.42	2.16	2.03	1.28	3.87
Completed college	1.60	1.37	2.17	2.04	6.84
Graduate work	0.98	0.83	2.34	3.66	6.83
73. Education of mother:					
Some high school	1.65	0.35	1.22	0.06	0.77
Completed high school	1.38	1.79	1.86	1.10	3.90
Some college	1.90	2.71	0.91	0.98	6.01
Completed college	1.31	0.85	2.65	2.26	6.14
Graduate work	0.00	0.00	0.00	0.49	1.21
74. Occupational classification of father:					
III. Skilled trades	1.83	3.17	2.36	1.57	1.04
II. Semiprofessional and managerial	2.30	2.32	1.61	0.39	7.74
I. Profession	1.27	2.03	2.94	4.63	10.50
75. Room-person ratio:					
1.50–1.74	3.20	2.67	0.10	0.51	5.16
1.75–1.99	1.04	0.37	2.37	1.02	3.71
2.00–2.24	2.95	1.88	0.34	2.22	2.86
2.25 and over	0.82	1.15	0.59	1.52	2.43

TABLE 5. — *Continued*

Environmental Item	Quin- tiles 1 and 2	Quin- tiles 2 and 3	Quin- tiles 3 and 4	Quin- tiles 4 and 5	Quin- tiles 1 and 5
76. Number of books in library:					
51–100..........................	2.87	2.79	1.29	1.52	2.84
101–250.........................	2.29	2.62	2.10	0.99	7.73
251–500.........................	1.28	1.14	2.92	0.98	5.41
77. Number of children's books:					
11–30...........................	4.10	2.22	2.25	2.72	1.67
31–50...........................	2.30	1.44	1.70	0.27	5.26
Over 50.........................	2.65	2.14	4.56	3.54	12.49
78. Number of magazines:					
4...............................	2.53	2.22	0.31	2.11	2.85
5...............................	2.83	2.04	0.17	0.91	3.89
6 and over......................	2.29	3.83	3.56	4.87	16.94
79. Cultural content score of magazines:					
20–29.9	0.00	5.89	0.94	0.94	6.79
30–39.9	0.00	1.59	1.37	4.73	7.38
40–49.9	0.00	0.00	2.66	1.34	3.72
50–59.9	0.00	0.00	1.55	1.43	2.78

phone, which differentiates all but the two highest quintiles. The discrimination between quintiles 1 and 5 for the entire list of items is sharp and definitely significant.

ITEMS ELIMINATED

The elimination of those items whose predictive value could not be substantiated by a mathematical constant is now clearly possible. A ratio for each quintile difference to its standard error of 2.0 or greater (i.e., 978 chances in 1,000 for a difference greater than zero, 22 for reversal) in three of the five comparisons was arbitrarily set as the criterion of retention for the alternate-response items. On this basis the following 24 items were eliminated:

1. Mother not employed
6. Home not connected with store
8. Parents not separated or divorced
14. Second automobile
15. Radio
21. Moving picture camera
28. Ventilating fan for kitchen
29. Desk in living room
30. Table lamps
31. Metropolitan newspaper other than local
32. Country or lake home
42. Trade union for father
47. University extension course for father
48. Professional or scientific society for mother
54. University extension course for mother
58. Horseback riding for either parent
61. Art lessons for child
62. Expression lessons for child
63. Foreign-language lessons for child
65. Pay clubs for child
67. Attend Sunday School for child
68. Attend movies for child
70. Regular allowance
71. Collections made by child

Four other items that met the standard outlined above (2, 3, 4, and 9) were dropped because of their lack of universality. To illustrate, because home ownership is not common in the densely populated cities, item 9, "Do not rent home," was eliminated. Again, authentic information relating to the items of relief and delinquency is available only in areas providing a social service exchange.

Further, the 6 items dependent on the investigator's judgment were omitted. In spite of their apparent differentiating ability, it was believed that without a comparative guide their retention only increased the unreliability of the final scale. All rating items are included here:

35. Home in good repair	82. Orderliness
80. Exterior of home	83. Good taste
81. Cleanliness	84. Condition of furnishings

Item 66, "leadership position for child," was eliminated because of the wide variation in definitions of a leadership position.

For the graduated items (72–79), the predictive standard described above was established for at least one of the levels of each item except 79, "cultural content score of magazines." Here, apparently, significant differences exist only between the extreme score groups. The fact of a positive correlation between occupational status and each of the graduated items was taken as evidence of their contribution to the total environmental complex. These correlation ratios are as follows:

Occupation and education of mother......... .64±.03
Occupation and room-person ratio........... .33±.02
Occupation and children's books .... .58±.02
Occupation and other books in library .... .66±.02
Occupation and number of magazines........ .64±.02
Occupation and cultural content score of magazines .... .64±.02

The 50 items retained for our final scale include the graduated ones, as indicated above, and all other factual non-rating items that were known to be universally applicable and that met the arbitrary standard for the differentiation of sub-score groups as defined.

AGE OF CHILD AND ITEMS SELECTED

Since, as has been said, certain material facilities of homes and certain community interests of parents seem contingent on the age of the children in the home, an analysis of the age of the children in our study was made. Clearly, if the children in our highest quintile groups were older on the average than those in our lowest quintiles, we might expect the respective scores of these quintiles to be definitely influenced by the factor of age. And hence the successive differences between quintiles would be due to differences in the age of child rather than to real differences in environment, so far as the family as a whole was concerned. As will be observed from the following tabulation, the agreement in the age of the children in the quintile groups is striking:

Quintile	Mean Age	Standard Deviation
1	10.5	2.73
2	10.0	2.61
3	10.0	2.53
4	10.1	2.66
5	9.6	2.53

It is apparent from these figures that age of child participating in the study does not explain the differences in score between our groups.

Still the possibility that the individual items are preferential to certain age levels is not removed. An unbalanced selection would destroy the general usefulness of our scale. That this possibility might be thoroughly explored, a study of total score according to age of children and a careful analysis of the separate items were undertaken.

Table 6 presents total scores for each age level. The differences in mean score are negligible. The five-year-olds have the lowest and

TABLE 6. — TOTAL SCORE TABULATED ACCORDING TO AGE OF CHILD
(Score computed by simple method.)

Age of Child *	Number of Cases	Mean Score	Standard Deviation	σm	σ Diff. between Successive Means	$\dfrac{D}{\sigma \text{ Diff.}}$
5.	19	36.2	14.9	3.4	. .	. .
6.	45	40.8	13.3	1.9	3.9	1.1
7.	72	44.4	13.4	1.6	2.5	1.4
8.	64	43.5	15.7	1.9	2.5	0.3
9.	60	39.8	14.3	1.9	2.7	1.3
10.	75	38.7	14.0	1.6	2.5	0.4
11.	72	41.6	15.8	1.9	2.5	1.2
12.	71	40.3	15.3	1.8	2.6	0.5
13.	66	40.4	13.3	1.6	2.4	0.0
14.	56	40.3	14.7	1.9	2.6	0.0

* Nearest year.

TABLE 7. — PERCENTAGE FREQUENCY OF OCCURRENCE OF CERTAIN ITEMS ACCORDING TO AGE OF CHILD INCLUDED IN STUDY

Age of Child *	Number of Children	Piano	Washing Machine	Folding Camera	Camp	Mother in P. T. A.	Music Lessons	Dancing Lessons	Dental Attention	Play Equipment	Nursery or Recreational Room	Bicycle or Tricycle	Encyclopedia	Typewriter
5	19	32	37	42	0	32	5	5	50	42	26	63	42	37
6	45	49	29	60	3	69	16	28	53	44	27	62	43	33
7	72	71	25	64	5	68	18	23	70	54	28	62	51	25
8	64	61	23	61	2	75	28	22	74	45	27	48	58	33
9	60	63	32	43	8	63	42	22	63	47	13	40	40	28
10	75	51	24	43	9	59	41	19	55	23	19	39	43	20
11	72	60	31	50	10	67	41	16	67	25	13	47	58	25
12	71	65	27	37	12	60	47	20	68	28	14	51	52	21
13	66	70	33	47	12	64	57	14	67	23	15	52	53	30
14	56	66	32	45	10	54	55	20	66	21	14	46	46	34

* Nearest year.

the seven-year-olds the highest score. The differences between the mean score of the six-year-olds and those of the eleven-, twelve-, thirteen-, and fourteen-year-olds are less than one. The differences between successive age levels are clearly not significant.

Table 7 shows the percentage frequency of occurrence, according to age, of specific items whose presence in homes might be a function of age. An analysis of the successive age groups shows no reliable differences except between the five- and six-year-olds in the case of "mother's membership in parent-teachers association," "music lessons," and "dancing lessons." The "piano," "mother in parent-teachers association," "dental attention," "encyclopedia," and "typewriter" show a slight but unreliable difference with age. A tendency toward a consistent increase with age is apparent for the items of "camps," "music lessons," and "dancing lessons." A reverse tendency, i. e., a decrease in occurrence, is evident in the case of the "folding camera," "playground equipment," "a nursery or recreational room," and "bicycle or tricycle." The magnitude of the difference between the youngest and oldest groups for any of the foregoing items is such that it would probably be maintained in another sampling of cases. Considering the scale as a whole, however, the items are apparently so balanced that no one age level is favored. The agreement observed in the mean scores of all the age levels demonstrates this fact. (See Table 6.)

V. A DESCRIPTION OF THE MINNESOTA HOME STATUS INDEX

CLASSIFICATION OF ITEMS

Once the items composing the scale were selected, the problem of their arrangement was in order. Two ideas dominated our consideration of this problem. It was believed desirable, first, that whatever form our classification took, it should facilitate the administration of the scale; second, that linkages or clusters of items used by earlier investigators should be adhered to wherever possible.

Despite the fact that facilitation in administration of any questionnaire is in large part a matter of the ability of the investigator, the order of the questions can considerably affect an instrument of the type presented in this study. The least personal questions should generally come first, the more personal questions later, after the investigator has gained the confidence of his respondent. Further, questions that might embarrass the informant should not come early in the interview; on the other hand, questions that people have been observed to enjoy should come early. On the basis of these hypotheses the section devoted to children's play and cultural materials is placed first in our questionnaire, and the amount of schooling of the parents is the last topic upon which interrogation is made.

In addition, the coherence of successive questions should always be a consideration. Clearly it is desirable to complete the questions relating to the electrical equipment of the home before undertaking an entirely different category of information. Although the sequence of our sections or indices and that of the questions within each index have been arbitrary, we have attempted to consider the relation of questionnaire reliability to completeness and accuracy of responses and hence have introduced what seemed most likely to bring about these ends. Other things being equal, a questionnaire that is so arranged as to increase the willingness of respondents to report facts completely and accurately will in all probability secure more reliable answers than one in which the order of presentation is given no consideration.

In assigning a question to a particular category or index two guides were used: first, the judgment of three persons presumably competent to judge* and, secondly, clusters used by earlier investigators. To classify books and magazines, for example, as indices of the cultural level of a home is purely arbitrary. Arguments could be advanced for their significance as economic indices. In the opinion of the judges and of previous investigators, however, these items are regarded as indications of the cultural level of a home. Our Economic Status indices correspond to McCormick's Material Status of the Home (29). Chapin's Group Setting Index, which appeared in one of his preliminary studies (6), is similar to our Sociality Index. Because Occupation and Education have been used as single indices in other investigations they are listed separately. Regardless of the fact that our classification is based on personal judgment, the grouping of parts into workable wholes or part-wholes is to be desired if on no other ground than utility. The value of the individual item has in no way been lost, since its score, which will be discussed later, was determined independently of its classification. Statistical support for the presence of item cleavage within our indices will be presented in Chapter VI.

Turning now to our scale (see pages 43–46), we may examine the classification of questions under specific indices and the order of the questions within the indices. No precise rules for the order of administration are laid down as they are in a well-standardized intelligence test. In the latter the questions are arranged in order of difficulty. In our questionnaire they are listed in order of probable degree of acceptability to the respondent. Because individuals and situations differ so greatly, an investigator should be ever on the alert to modify the order of administration if in his opinion a different order of questioning would result in greater willingness to disclose the facts.

An Examination of the Index

As will be seen upon an examination of the Index, the form of question used in the original schedule has been retained. The classification of the questions, however, is for the most part new. Six categories of questions that summate what evidence we have for the abstract concepts expressed in the captions — Children's Facilities, Economic Status, Cultural Status, Sociality, Occupational Status, and Educational Status — are listed as given. The number of specific items in each category varies from 1 in Occupational

---

* Florence L. Goodenough, psychologist, Institute of Child Welfare, University of Minnesota; Marjorie Shaw, social investigator, Institute of Child Welfare, University of Minnesota; and the author.

Status to 13 in Economic Status and Sociality. The score values attached to each question will be discussed presently. The directions for recording replies are stated at the beginning of the scale proper. Under "General Information" space has been allowed for the kind of data usually desired when making a study of a home in reference to a particular child. The Score Summary needs no elaboration. The method by which the scores were computed will be presented in detail. Table 10 is used in converting the raw scores of the indices into their sigma equivalents. The Home Status Profile below permits a graphic representation of the score obtained by a home. This should prove helpful in individualizing the home of a particular child. In research studies, however, this section would probably have less value. The Home Status indices appear next and in the following order: Children's Facilities, Economic Status, Cultural Status, Sociality, Occupational Status, and Educational Status. As previously described, each is composed of a series of direct questions. These are self-explanatory. The scores given the replies and the various methods employed in scoring will be discussed presently.

Scoring the Questions

The numerical values attached to the *yes* and *no* replies of the alternative-response questions and to the various degrees of the graduated items shown in the previous section constitute the score that the items are to receive. These respective values were assigned after careful consideration of several possible scoring methods.

The first method considered is commonly known as the *simple method*. Here zero is assigned to the absence of the item or factor and 1 to its presence. In the case of graduated items, such as education, multiple values of 1 are given for successive levels of the factor. There is no consideration of whether or not the successive levels are equally spaced. The entire scheme is an arbitrary assignment of number values. Its only merit lies in the simplicity of its determination. In these data, as will be subsequently shown, the method yields as good results as do methods whose computation is exceedingly more difficult.

The second method employed is equally arbitrary. For convenience we shall refer to it as the *difference method* because its values were based on the reliability of the percentage differences of possession existing between subclasses of the entire population. The score for each item was the average of the ratios of the differences to their standard errors. Since there were five subgroup comparisons in the analysis of each question, the item score may be expressed as follows:

$$\frac{\Sigma \dfrac{D}{\sigma \text{ diff.}}}{5}$$

As is evident, values thus assigned reflect all that underlies the determination of the significance of a difference. A normal distribution is assumed, and the score is in direct relation to the magnitude of the ratio between a difference and its standard error. Obviously the basis of significance in such a weighting scheme is not the frequency of occurrence of the item in the entire population but the magnitude of the difference in occurrence in relation to its standard error between subdivisions of the total population. Whether the 120 cases in each quintile group fairly represent the homes of the general population may be seriously questioned. Although our total number of cases is an attempted random sampling, neither this sub-sample nor any other group similarly selected, and approximately of the same size, will represent the entire population perfectly. The merit of this method in data employing the test of internal consistency as a discriminating device lies not only in the importance attached to the stability of the difference between segments of the distribution but also in its ease of calculation.

The third method employed and the one accepted for use in our scale is generally known as the *sigma method of scoring*. The weight given an item is in inverse relation to its frequency in the total population. Items that occur rarely are given the greatest weight, and absence or nonpossession of an item, as well as presence or possession of it, receives a score value. As in the difference method, each item is assumed to be normally distributed. In addition, when, as in this study, the possession of an item is regarded as desirable, there is the assumption that possession deviates on the positive side of the mean of the whole distribution with 100 per cent as its termination point. On the other hand nonpossession of the item deviates in a negative direction from the mean of the whole distribution with the 50th percentile as its termination point. Furthermore, it posits that the most typical figure for percentage of either possession or nonpossession is one-half the observed percentage frequency.

THE MINNESOTA HOME STATUS INDEX: A SCALE FOR MEASURING URBAN HOME ENVIRONMENT

No............................ Date.......................... Total Raw Score...............................

Interviewer .... Average Sigma Score................................

GENERAL INFORMATION

Name of family..

Street address..Telephone No..

City or place..

Person interviewed: Mother.. Father..

Other adult................................... Child...................................
relation to family

Name of child...

Sex: M............ F............

Date of Birth: Year............................... Month.......................... Day...............................

Age: Years.................. Months.................... School Grade.................... IQ..................

Other living children: Number of boys older...............Number of girls older...............

Number of boys younger............Number of girls younger ....

Total number of children in family............

Others in household: Father............Mother............

Number of relatives............ Number of roomers............

SCORE SUMMARY

Home Status Indices	Score Range	Raw Score	Sigma Score of Indices
I. Children's Facilities Index........:.	33–66	....	....
II. Economic Status Index............	36–77	....	....
III. Cultural Status Index.............	30–68	....	....
IV. Sociality Index...................	38–75	....	....
V. Occupational Status Index........	1–8	....	....
VI. Educational Status Index..........	2–8	....	....

Directions. — The answers to the questions listed below provide a quantitative description of home equipment and family life. Circle the correct answer to each question. "Y" is an abbreviation for "yes" and the number under it is its score value. "N" is an abbreviation for "no" and the number under it is its score value. Some of the questions have a choice of several answers, for example, the question relative to the number of children's books in the home. In answering this question you must circle one of four possible replies. Be sure to circle only one answer for each question. When all the questions have been answered, place the score in the space to the left of each question. Total each section or index separately and then transfer these figures to the space allowed under the heading "Score Summary." Neither the order of questions within an index nor the order of indices as printed need be followed in the interview. They are only suggestive. However, experience indicates that the order given should generally facilitate the collection of the data.

How to score omissions. — Intentional or accidental omissions should be scored as follows. Compute the total score for the questions answered in the section in which the omissions occur. Divide this total by the number of questions answered in the section. The quotient thus obtained will constitute the best probable score to give each omitted question in the section involved. Repeat the same for each section in which omissions occur.

I. CHILDREN'S FACILITIES INDEX

SCORE		Yes	No
....	1. Does family have two or more pieces of playground equipment?	6	3
....	2. Does child have bicycle or tricycle?	5	3
....	3. Is there a nursery or recreational room?	7	4
....	4. Has child had paid lessons in music outside of school?	6	3
....	5. Has child had paid lessons in dancing outside of school?..	7	4
....	6. Is child given a certain amount of money regularly to spend?..	6	3
....	7. Does child have an account in a public or school bank?	5	2
....	8. Has child ever belonged to any paid clubs or groups?	6	3
....	9. Did child go to a boys (or girls) camp this summer or last summer?	7	4
....	10. Has child been to dentist within past year?	5	2
....	11. About how many children's books are there in the home?		

	Number:	0–10	11–30	31–50	over 50
	Score:	2	4	5	6

.... TOTAL SCORE

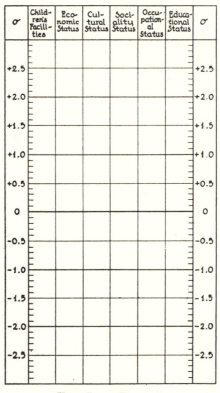

σ	Child-ren's Facili-ties	Eco-nomic Status	Cul-tural Status	Soci-ality Status	Occu-pation-al Status	Educa-tional Status	σ
+2.5							+2.5
+2.0							+2.0
+1.5							+1.5
+1.0							+1.0
+0.5							+0.5
0							0
-0.5							-0.5
-1.0							-1.0
-1.5							-1.5
-2.0							-2.0
-2.5							-2.5

HOME STATUS PROFILE *

* The profile gives a graphic picture of the standing of a home in relation to the average home located at zero sigma for each categorical index. To construct a profile first convert the raw scores listed above into sigma equivalents as given in Table 10.

II. Economic Status Index

		Score for:	
Score		Yes	No
....	1. Are there stores in the same block with the home?............	4	7
....	2. Is either of the following within one-fourth mile of the home: factory or warehouse?.................................	2	5
	Are the following facilities provided?		
....	3. Central heating system.................................	5	2
....	4. A second bathroom or more.............................	7	4
....	5. Telephone	5	2
....	6. Vacuum cleaner..	5	2
....	7. Washing machine and mangle.............................	6	3
....	8. Electric refrigerator	6	3
....	9. Does family have an automobile?.........................	5	2
....	10. Does family have a boat?................................	7	4
....	11. Did family go away for a vacation within the past year?......	5	2
....	12. Is there any paid assistance in the home?...................	6	3
....	13. Room-person ratio..		

Divide number of rooms by persons

Ratio	Score
.25–1.49..................................	3
1.5 –1.99..................................	5
2.0 –2.24..................................	6
2.25–3.25..................................	8

How many rooms?
Number 1 2 3 4 5 6 7 8 9 10
How many people in the home?.................

.... **Total Score**

III. Cultural Status Index

		Score for:	
Score		Yes	No
	Does family have a:		
....	1. Folding camera?...	5	3
....	2. Typewriter at home?.....................................	6	3
....	3. Fireplace?	6	3
....	4. Piano?	5	2
....	5. Encyclopedia?	5	3
....	6. Does either parent play a musical instrument?..............	5	2
....	7. Has father been a member of a professional or scientific society?	6	3

.... 8. How many daily papers are taken?

Number:	0–1	2	3 and over
Score:	3	6	8

.... 9. How many magazines are regularly taken in the home? *

Number:	0–3	4–5	3 and over
Score:	3	5	6

.... 10. What is cultural content score of magazines? †

Ratings	Score
0– 9.9..................................	2
10–19.9..................................	4
20–29.9..................................	5
30–39.9..................................	6
40–59.9..................................	8

What are the names of the magazines?.................................

.... 11. About how many books other than children's are in the home?

Number:	0–50	51–250	250–500	Over 500
Score:	3	5	7	8

.... **Total Score**

* By *regularly* is meant as frequently as the magazine is published.
† Ratings for general interest magazines are given in Table 9 on p. 50.

IV. Sociality Index

SCORE		Yes	No
	Has father been a member of a:		
....	1. Fraternal society?	5	3
....	2. Social club?	5	3
....	3. Parent-teachers association?	6	3
....	4. Civic or political club?	6	3
....	5. Study club, literary or art society?	7	4
	Has mother been a member of a:		
....	6. Fraternal society?	6	3
....	7. Social club?	5	3
....	8. Parent-teachers association?	5	2
....	9. Civic or political club?	7	3
....	10. Study club, literary or art society?	6	3
	Does either parent participate in any of the following forms of recreation:		
....	11. Fishing or hunting?	5	2
....	12. Bridge?	5	3
....	13. Tennis or golf?	6	3
....	TOTAL SCORE		

V. Occupational Status Index

What is father's usual occupation?..

* Scale:	VII Day labor	VI Slightly skilled	V Semi-skilled	III Skilled trades	II Semi-professional and managerial	I Profession
Score:	1	2	4	5	7	8

............Score

* F. L. Goodenough and J. E. Anderson. *Experimental Child Study* (The Century Co., New York, 1931), pp. 501–12.

VI. Educational Status Index (Midparent Education *)

	SCORE
What was the school attainment of the father?	
8th grade or less	2
Entered high school	4
Completed high school	5
Entered college	5
Completed college	6
Graduate work	7
What was the school attainment of the mother?	
8th grade or less	2
Entered high school	4
Completed high school	5
Entered college	6
Completed college	7
Graduate work	9

............Total Score *

* This is the sum of the education score of both parents divided by two. When the education of only one parent is known, it should be accepted as the probable school attainment of both parents.

The calculation of the sigma score for an item such as central heating system, which was possessed by 78.2 per cent and absent in 21.8 per cent of the homes, would proceed as follows:

$$\frac{100-78.2=60.9}{2}$$

The distance of 60.9 per cent from the mean (50.0 per cent), which is +.266 sigmas, may be read from a table of the normal probability curve.* This, then, constitutes the score for those homes possessing a central heating system. The calculation of the score to be given the homes that do not possess a central heating system would be computed as follows: first determine the typical value of the observed frequency, which in this instance is 21.8÷2, or 10.9; then, regarding the 50th percentile as the termination point for this segment of the distribution, the sigma value of 10.9 per cent is read directly from a table of normal probability. This gives −1.2 sigmas as the score for the absence of a central heating system.

Each question or item retained for the Index was treated thus. In the case of categorical and graduated items it was necessary to determine the cumulative percentage frequency distribution of the item and then regard the end of each successive truncated section as the termination point from which the typical value would be located. For example, the categories of a percentage distribution such as listed below would have the sigma values recorded in the extreme right-hand column.

Category	Percentage Frequency	Cumulative Percentage Frequency	Sigma Values
I	4.2	100.0	+1.96
II	9.6	95.8	+1.31
III	22.0	86.2	+ .66
IV	42.6	64.2	− .16
V	8.2	21.6	− .94
VI	13.4	13.4	−1.48

Finally, from scores expressed in equivalent sigma units, some of which were positive and some negative, the scores attached to the items already shown in our Index were computed. To avoid the negative signs of the original sigma scores, 2 was added to all sigma values. To increase the magnitude of our figures, all were multiplied by 2. These results were then expressed to the nearest whole number as our final scores.

* E. L. Thorndike. *Mental and Social Measurements* (Teachers College, Columbia University, New York, 1904), p. 217, table 48.

	Simple Method		Difference Method		Sigma Method	
	Yes	No	Yes	No	Yes	No

CHILDREN'S FACILITIES INDEX

Playground equipment (2 pieces or more)?	1	0	6	0	6	3
Bicycle or tricycle for child?	1	0	5	0	5	3
Nursery or recreational room?	1	0	4	0	7	4
Has child had paid lessons in music outside of school?	1	0	4	0	6	3
Has child had paid lessons in dancing outside of school?	1	0	3	0	7	4
Is child given a certain amount of money regularly to spend?	1	0	3	0	6	3
Does child have an account in a public or school bank?	1	0	4	0	5	2
Has child ever belonged to any paid clubs or groups?	1	0	2	0	6	3
Did child go to a boys (or girls) camp this summer or last summer?	1	0	2	0	7	4
Has child been to dentist within past year?	1	0	5	0	5	2

ECONOMIC STATUS INDEX

Are there stores in the same block with the home?	1	0	5	0	4	7
Is either of the following within one-fourth mile of the home: factory or warehouse?	1	0	3	0	2	5
Are the following facilities provided:						
Central heating system?	1	0	6	0	5	2
A second bathroom or more?	1	0	3	0	7	4
Telephone?	1	0	9	0	5	2
Vacuum cleaner?	1	0	8	0	5	2
Washing machine and mangle?	1	0	3	0	6	3
Electric refrigerator?	1	0	5	0	6	3
Does family have an automobile?	1	0	7	0	5	2
Does family have a boat?	1	0	2	0	7	4
Did family go away for a vacation within the past year?	1	0	2	0	5	2
Is there any paid assistance in the home?	1	0	6	0	6	3

CULTURAL STATUS INDEX

Does family have a:						
Folding camera?	1	0	6	0	5	3
Typewriter at home?	1	0	4	0	6	3
Fireplace?	1	0	7	0	6	3
Piano?	1	0	5	0	5	2
Encyclopedia?	1	0	6	0	5	3
Does either parent play a musical instrument?	1	0	3	0	5	2
Has father been a member of a professional club or scientific society?	1	0	5	0	6	3

SOCIALITY INDEX

Has father been a member of:						
A fraternal society?	1	0	3	0	5	3
Social club?	1	0	6	0	5	3
A parent-teachers association?	1	0	4	0	6	3
Civic or political club?	1	0	4	0	6	3
Study club, literary or art society?	1	0	3	0	7	4

TABLE 8. — *Continued*

	Sigma Method		Difference Method		Simple Method	
	Yes	No	Yes	No	Yes	No
Has mother been a member of:						
A fraternal society?	1	0	2	0	6	3
Social club?	1	0	6	0	5	3
A parent-teachers association?	1	0	6	0	5	2
Civic or political club?	1	0	3	0	7	3
Study club, literary or art society?	1	0	5	0	6	3
Does either parent participate in:						
Fishing or hunting?	1	0	4	0	5	2
Bridge?	1	0	7	0	5	2
Tennis or golf?	1	0	6	0	6	3

In Table 8 are presented the item scores computed according to each of the three methods just described. Although different absolute values are assigned by the three methods, the relative total score of a home is identical on all three methods, judging from the correlations which follow:

.99±.00 for simple and difference method on entire sample of 600 homes.
.98±.00 for simple and sigma method on standard sample of 200 homes.
.98±.00 for sigma and difference method on standard sample of 200 homes.

Apparently the three methods of scoring are equally good. Differences in absolute weights are seemingly due to methods of computation rather than to any real differences in the facts they are intended to set forth. Clearly the only claim to superiority that can be made for the sigma method of scoring is that it can be expressed in a universally understandable unit.

Scoring Omissions

On the theory that a part score is indicative of the whole, the following correction for omissions is proposed: (1) divide the score received in each section by the number of questions answered and (2) assign this quotient as the score value of each of the omitted questions.

For example, if questions 9 (automobile) and 8 (electric refrigerator) of the Economic Status Index are omitted in the survey of a particular home and on the remaining eleven questions in that category the home receives a score of 58, then the score to be assigned each omitted question is 58÷11, or 5.3. Thus the corrected score will not be as low as if omissions were regarded as nonpossession nor as high as if credit for possession were given. Although this method provides only a crude approximation, it is believed that no serious harm is done when a large number of homes are under consideration. In all probability some of the homes will possess the omitted items, whereas others will not. Ideally, answers to all the questions should be sought for every home included in an investigation.

TABLE 9. — CULTURAL WEIGHTS OF GENERAL INTEREST MAGAZINES *

Weight	Magazine	Weight	Magazine
10	Yale Review Atlantic Monthly Saturday Review of Literature		Popular Science Popular Mechanics Saturday Evening Post Ladies' Home Journal
9	Bookman Nation Forum Harper's New Republic	5	Life Woman's Home Companion Delineator Collier's Pictorial Review Pathfinder Judge American Magazine
8	Living Age Current History American Mercury Asia Survey National Geographic Scribner's Scientific Monthly	4	McCall's Cosmopolitan Redbook Adventure Liberty
7	World's Work Review of Reviews Scientific American Golden Book Outlook Literary Digest Travel Time House Beautiful Fortune Reader's Digest	3	Argosy College Humor Physical Culture
6	House and Garden Nation's Business Better Homes and Gardens New Yorker Parents' Magazine Hygeia Field and Stream Vanity Fair Theatre Magazine Harper's Bazaar Country Gentleman Good Housekeeping Vogue	2	Photoplay Motion Picture Magazine Sport Story Magazine Real Detective Stories Detective Story Magazine Short Stories Film Fun Western Story Complete Story
		1	Love Story Magazine Breezy Stories Screen Secrets True Story True Confessions

* Taken from W. L. Morgan and A. M. Leahy. "The Cultural Content of General Interest Magazines," *Journal of Educational Psychology,* 25:534 (October, 1934).

TABLE 10. — CONVERSION TABLE OF TOTAL SCORES OF INDICES INTO SIGMA SCORES

Sigma Score	Children's Facilities Index	Economic Status Index	Cultural Status Index	Sociality Index	Occupational Status Index	Educational Status Index
2.9	66					
2.8						
2.7	65			75		
2.6	64		68	74		
2.5			67	73		8
2.4	63		66	72		
2.3	62	77	65			
2.2	61	76	64	71		7.5
2.1		75	63	70		
2.0	60		62	69		
1.9	59	74	61	68		7
1.8	58	73	60	67		
1.7		72	59	66		
1.6	57	71	58	65		6.5
1.5	56	70	57	64		
1.4	55	69	56		8	
1.3		68	55	63		6
1.2	54	67	54	62		
1.1	53	66		61		
1.0		65	53	60	7	5.5
.9	52	64	52	59		
.8	51	63	51	58		5
.7	50	62	50	57		
.6		61	49			
.5	49	60	48	56		4.5
.4	48	59	47	55		
.3		58	46	54		
.2	47	57	45	53		
.1	46	56	44	52		
.0	45	55	43	51	5	4
— .1			42	50		
— .2	44	54	41	49	4	3.5
— .3	43	53	40			
— .4	42	52	39	48		
— .5		51	38	47		3
— .6	41	50		46		
— .7	40	49	37	45		
— .8		48	36	44		2.5
— .9	39	47	35	43		
—1.0	38	46	34	42		
—1.1	37	45	33	41		2
—1.2		44	32		2	
—1.3	36	43	31	40		
—1.4	35	42	30	39		
—1.5	34	41		38		
—1.6		40				
—1.7	33	39				
—1.8		38			1	
—1.9						
—2.0		37				
—2.1		36				

CULTURAL CONTENT SCORE OF MAGAZINES

Question 9 in the Cultural Status Index above calls for the number of magazines taken by the family, and question 10 for a cultural content score for the magazines. The scale devised for the latter, which is reproduced in Table 9, is taken from a study entitled "The Cultural Content of General Interest Magazines" by W. L. Morgan and the writer (30).

General interest magazines that do not appear in the list may be given the scores of similar magazines that are in the scale, or question 10 may be omitted. Neither its inclusion and expansion nor its omission would affect the relative position of any one home in a research study, so long as the procedure is consistent throughout the entire population. A consideration of the number of magazines in a home has characterized all modern home rating devices. This scale is the first, however, to attempt an evaluation of the type of magazine found in the home.

HOME STATUS PROFILE

Attention should be called to the chart on page 44, entitled Home Status Profile. It will be noted that the extreme left-hand column constitutes a rule of equally spaced positive and negative sigma positions from zero. The horizontal line at zero represents the sigma position of the mean. On either side of the latter may be drawn the sigma levels of the scores attained in any or all of the indices of our scale. As may be seen from the captions across the top, a column is allowed for each index.

So that the indices could be graphically represented as the chart above provides, all possible total scores for the separate indices were converted into sigma scores. These are presented in Table 10. In the construction of this table the mean and standard deviation of each index attribute was determined for our entire population of six hundred homes. Then the distance from the mean in sigma or standard deviation units was calculated for each possible score. The process may be expressed thus:

$$\frac{\bar{X} - X}{\sigma}$$

The chief use of the profile is in the diagnosis of individual homes. Foster homes, homes of delinquents, and the homes of other persons receiving individual attention might profitably be plotted. In clinical diagnosis and guidance it should be a distinct help. The profile shows clearly the position of a home in relation to the average home of our population. To the extent that we have a fair sample of urban homes, it shows the relation of any single home to urban homes in general; to the extent that the items composing our indices fairly sample all possible indicators of the general attribute in question, it shows the relation of any single home to the generality for the attribute under consideration.

VI. AN EVALUATION OF THE MINNESOTA HOME STATUS INDEX

Up to this point we have been describing the procedure by which the Minnesota Home Status Index was constructed. It has been shown how each item was tested to establish its value as a part of the scale, how from this information a group of items was chosen, then classified, and how each item was weighted for scoring. Finally, it was shown how to combine these scores to make a total score expressing a family's environmental status.

The merit of the scale as a whole will now be discussed. The question of its reliability will be considered, then the contribution of its several parts to the whole, and finally its validity. The use of the Index and problems for further study will also be considered.

THE RELIABILITY OF THE MINNESOTA INDEX

The accuracy with which our Index measures that which it has been designed to measure might be determined in three different ways: (1) by repeating the scale after an interval of time has elapsed; (2) by the simultaneous administration of the scale by two different investigators; and (3) by correlating half of the scale with the other half.

In all three methods the magnitude of the coefficient of correlation is the measure of reliability. If it is high, the scale is said to be reliable; if it is low, it is not reliable. The first two methods permit higher correlations than does the third. Increased heterogeneity due to variation in conditions at the time of the administration of the scale is possible when the first method is used. Differences peculiar to investigators increase the spread in the second method. In the third method the extent to which the halves are noncomparable lowers the correlation, since this method presupposes that the parts are exactly comparable. With data such as ours, exact comparability is not possible. For example, if the radio and the piano are selected as balanced items, one appearing in scale A, let us say, and the other in scale B, it does not follow that the presence or absence of these items will appear simultaneously in the same home.

A home rated by the first half of the scale may secure a high score and yet score comparatively low on the second half because of the nonequivalence of the items composing the respective scales. In mental tests, where this method is in common use, item equivalence is not affected by concrete existence but only by the failure to include in the scale a wide range of items covering any one aspect of intelligence. In spite of the limitations of the split-scale method of determining reliability, only this method was used because of lack of time. By the Spearman-Brown formula, reliability thus obtained was 0.92. This figure is lower than what might have been obtained if it had not been for the factors cited above, and if reliability had been based on the entire 50 items of the scale instead of on only 48 of them. Occupation and midparent education, both of which contribute considerably to our total score, were omitted in the process of splitting the scale. The halves were made only from those indices composed of multiple items. When all the conditions of our computation are taken into consideration, it appears that the scale is fairly reliable.

Also, it compares favorably with other scales as to reliability. Chapman and Sims reported 0.77 by the method of split halves and the Spearman-Brown formula. By the same method, Sims secured 0.91, Heilman 0.87, McCormick 0.96, and Burdick 0.50. By the method of simultaneous ratings Chapin reports 0.90 and by test-retest 0.98 for his Social Status Scale on a sample of 50 cases.

Contribution of Indices to Whole Scale

Do the separate indices make an independent contribution to the whole scale? Or, reversing the question, Does any one of them duplicate the others? Perfect agreement and, in consequence, exact duplication may be inferred to be present when an index or subscale correlates 1.0 with another. Where such duplication occurs, one of the items should be dropped. Certainly there is no advantage in using fifty questions if a smaller number give the same result.

Judging from the magnitude of the product moment correlations presented in Table 11, it appears that none of the indices are duplicates. Since, however, chance inaccuracies in our measures would tend to reduce these correlations toward zero, the correction for attenuation must be applied to each coefficient before its independent character may be judged.

TABLE 11. — INTERCORRELATIONS OF THE SEPARATE INDICES

	Economic (II)	Cultural (III)	Sociality (IV)	Occupational (V)	Educational (VI)
I. Children's Facilities Index	.61	.65	.61	.54	.47
II. Economic Status Index		.73	.66	.57	.71
III. Cultural Status Index			.67	.72	.69
IV. Sociality Index				.63	.62
V. Occupational Status Index					.59

In correcting for this decrease or attenuation of a coefficient, Spearman's formula as presented in Kelley was used:

$$r\infty\ \infty = \frac{r\ 12}{\sqrt{r_{1I}}\ \sqrt{r_{2II}}}$$

As is apparent in this formula, the reliability of the correlated indices must be determined. According to the split-scale method, using the Spearman-Brown prophecy formula, they are as follows:

Children's Facilities Index...................... 0.67
Economic Status Index 0.82
Cultural Status Index......................... 0.80
Sociality Index............................... 0.73

Because our Occupational and Educational Status indices consisted of a single factor, their reliabilities could not be determined. In view of their verifiable character, however, it is quite probable that higher coefficients of reliability by the test-retest method would be obtained for them than was secured for the other indices. Completing the process of correction for the remaining indices, we have the new coefficients presented in Table 12.

TABLE 12. — INTERCORRELATION OF INDICES CORRECTED FOR ATTENUATION

	Economic (II)	Cultural (III)	Sociality (IV)
I. Children's Facilities Index	.82	.89	.87
II. Economic Status Index		.90	.85
III. Cultural Status Index			.88

When allowance is thus made for inaccuracies of administration, errors of observation, and variation in our respondents, the intercorrelations of the indices, or subscales, increases from a range of .61–73 to .82–.90. The latter coefficients represent the relationship more exactly and, although noticeably increased, the error in estimating the score of one index from that of another would range

from about 40 to 60 per cent (coefficient of alienation $= 1 - \sqrt{1 - r^2}$).
From this it follows that no index entirely duplicates another and
that each is making an independent contribution to the whole scale.
Or we may conclude that the whole scale is broader than any one
of its parts.

Validity of the Index

Does our Index actually differentiate homes with respect to ex-
ternal environmental factors? If it does, we may say that it is a
valid measure of that which it purports to measure. A partial answer to the question might be found in the degree of similarity
existing between an already established measure of home differences and the Index. Correlation of the scores earned by the Index
with those given by the Sims Score Card in a sample of 200 homes
yielded a product moment coefficient of correlation of $+.94$. To the
extent that the Sims scale is a valid measure of home background,
we may say that the Index is virtually equally so.

A second attempt to determine the differentiating ability of the
Index was made by comparing the scores earned by two widely
different sets of homes. The homes chosen were those of professional men (doctors, lawyers, university teachers, etc.) and those of
day laborers. An inspection of Table 13, which presents the scores

TABLE 13. — COMPARISON OF SCORES OF CONTRASTED POPULATION GROUPS
(Scores calculated by simple method.)

	Occupational Group I			Occupational Group VII			Comparison	Chance in 1,000 of true difference greater than zero
	Number of Cases	Mean Score	Standard Deviation	Number of Cases	Mean Score	Standard Deviation	Critical Ratio D σ diff.	
Children's Facilities..	93	29.86	3.02	51	7.26	1.84	57.34	1,000
Economic Status. ...	93	50.78	1.61	51	9.66	1.88	129.30	1,000
Cultural Status	93	46.77	2.66	51	5.64	0.84	138.88	1,000
Sociality	92	37.83	2.83	51	6.00	1.25	93.34	1,000
Educational Status ..	94	15.24	1.84	37	5.69	3.39	11.67	1,000

of these populations, shows them to be definitely contrasted. In all
the indices except that of education the highest score earned in
the day labor group is lower than the lowest score of the professional group. The average midparent educational level of the professional group was attained but not surpassed by any individuals
in the day labor group. The probability that the differences between

the professional and the day labor group on any one index is not a matter of chance may be seen by the ratio of the difference to the sigma of its unreliability. For all indices it is more than three times as large as the sigma of its unreliability — the standard to which one usually adheres. From this evidence it would appear that the scale discriminates effectively between homes generally conceded to be widely separated.

The foregoing demonstrates that the Index has a certain practical validity on two counts: first, its measurements are consistent with the measurements of the same homes made with another scale, and, secondly, it keeps widely contrasted groups separated.

A comparison with the validity offered for other measures of home environment is satisfactory. Chapin (8), when he correlated his Living Room Scale with the Sims Score Card (34), secured a coefficient of +.69. When he used Holley's scale (24), the coefficient of correlation was +.51. Neither Sims' (34) nor McCormick's (29) scale was validated against other scales.

USES OF THE INDEX

As suggested in Chapter I, the need of measures such as the Index is clear. Progress in our ability to predict and control human behavior will be made only as we are able to create new measures or to improve and extend our already existing measures of those factors that are believed to be causative of human conduct.

The idea implicit in the Index is not new, nor is the method which it incorporates. The fact that it is an improvement over already existing measures is attested in our discussion of reliability.

But, aside from whatever merit it may have in respect to reliability, is not the Index merely duplicating that which is already being done by Sims' measure? It will be recalled that the two measures correlate +.94. A comparison of the two scales gives a negative answer. The Sims Score Card was standardized on and designed for older children whose reading comprehension is at least of sixth-grade level. This limits it to the homes of children who are about 11 years of age or older. The modern trend, however, from the standpoint of both research and service, is toward the study of the young child. The Index was standardized on children whose ages ranged from 5 to 14 years inclusive. Thus it covers the age group on which the Sims Score Card was standardized and extends downward to the 4-year level.

Since the young child is not a reliable informant of his home con-

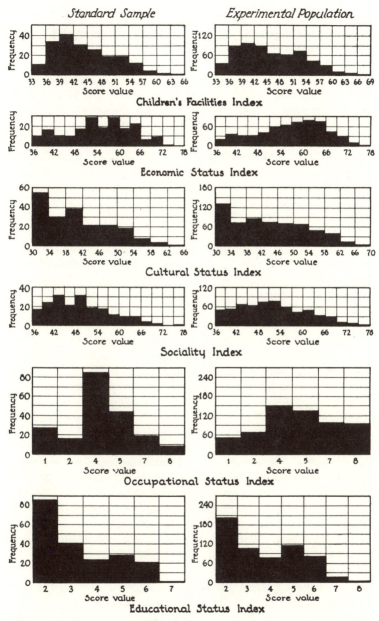

Figure 3. — Distribution of Index Scores of Standard Sample ($N = 200$) Compared with Those of the Total Experimental Population ($N = 600$). Areas Have Been Equated.

ditions, it follows that the information for the Index must be obtained from the parent. Not only is there a probable increase in reliability when such data are collected directly in the home, as is demanded by the Index, but the method is not as difficult as it appears. Many agencies and institutions making a study of children demand that the child's home be known at first hand. This is particularly true of all social work agencies, such as child-placement bureaus, child-guidance clinics, juvenile courts, and visiting teachers. This standard is held also by research and educational institutions, such as nursery schools and universities. Except in the universities, the administration of the Index would rarely involve any effort in addition to that demanded by the ordinary procedures of these organizations.

PROBLEMS FOR FURTHER STUDY

An examination of the Index and similar scales shows the effect of time and place upon measures of home environment. Certainly the differentiating significance of specific items of material equipment changes with time and place. What is rare today may be common in a decade or less. What is peculiarly significant in a given region may have little or no significance in others. For example, electric lights would have set a home apart from the average in 1900; today they are a common possession. Further, a central heating system in a home in southern California may reasonably be taken as an index of superior economic status, whereas it would not be so regarded in a north-temperate climate. Moreover, "place" with respect to rural or urban situation, while it continues to differentiate homes in most areas, is becoming less important, for modern invention is making the farm home increasingly similar to the city home. The revision of environmental scales to keep them up to date and the use of separate forms for different types of community appear to be a necessity. Certainly measures such as this Index should be tested for content against older ones. In all probability, certain items are less affected by time than others. Whether or not there is a body of facts that have a relatively constant capacity to differentiate homes would be interesting and valuable knowledge.

An additional problem of considerable significance is the true distribution of any one item or combination of items composing an environmental scale. Figure 3 shows the score distributions of the indices of our scale for our entire population and also for a sample population selected at random as male occupations are distributed in the general population. The similarity of the distributions in both populations is striking. In the main, the curves are negatively accelerated, and although no inference can be drawn as to their probable distribution in the general population, it is clear that the disproportion of occupations in our total group has not tended to distort the general character of the scores. The ease with which low occupational groups can secure a high score suggests the desirability of further testing and possibly the elimination of items now included in the scale. The point that is clearly demonstrated in these figures is our success in getting an unbiased sample of home differences as reflected by occupational status.

Summary

The present investigation used the interview method to collect information from at least one parent and one child in six hundred different urban homes concerning the material equipment of the home and the participation of the parents and the child in activities outside the home. An attempt was made to secure a fair sample of the homes of every occupational level. Following the classification proposed by Goodenough and Anderson (21), each occupational class was represented by fifty or more homes.

In addition to general identifying data the experimental schedules included 84 questions. The replies to these questions were first analyzed on the basis of percentage responding to every question. Then, following the method known as the "criterion of internal consistency," questions that were found to differentiate subgroups of the entire population were assigned score values according to the sigma method. Finally, the questions so selected and weighted were classified under one of the following indices: Children's Facilities, Economic Status, Cultural Status, Sociality, Occupational Status, or Educational Status.

The reliability was found by the method of split halves to be 0.92. Validity was measured by the correlation of the Index with the Sims scale as 0.94.

BIBLIOGRAPHY

1. Atwater, W. O. Principles of nutrition and nutritive value of food (United States Department of Agriculture, Farmers' Bulletin No. 142). Government Printing Office, 1910. 48 pp.
2. Barr, F. E. A scale for measuring mental ability in vocations and some of its applications. Unpublished master's thesis, Stanford University, 1918. Described in Lewis M. Terman, Genetic studies of genius, 1:66–72. Stanford University Press, 1925.
3. Burdick, Edith Marie. A group test of home environment (Archives of Psychology, No. 101). Columbia University, 1928. 115 pp.
4. Chapin, F. Stuart. Measuring the volume of social stimuli. Social Forces, 4:479–95 (1926).
5. ————. A quantitative scale for rating the home and social environment of middle class families in an urban community. Journal of Educational Psychology, 19:99–111 (1928).
6. ————. The measurement of sociability and socio-economic status. Sociology and Social Research, 12:208–17 (1928).
7. ————. A home rating scale to check social workers' opinions. Sociology and Social Research, 14:10–16 (1929).
8. ————. Scale for rating living room equipment (Institute of Child Welfare Circular No. 3). University of Minnesota, January, 1930.
9. ————. Socio-economic status: some preliminary results of measurement. American Journal of Sociology, 37:581–87 (January, 1932).
10. ————. The measurement of social status. University of Minnesota Press, 1933. 15 pp.
11. Chapman, J. Crosby, and V. M. Sims. The quantitative measurement of certain aspects of socio-economic status. Journal of Educational Psychology, 16:380–90 (1925).
12. Commons, J. R. Standardization of housing investigations. Journal of the American Statistical Association, 2:319–26 (1908).
13. Counts, George S. The selective character of American secondary education (Supplementary Education Monograph No. 19). University of Chicago Press, 1922. 156 pp.
14. Cuff, N. B. Relationship of socio-economic status to intelligence and achievement. Peabody Journal of Education, 11:106–10 (1933).
15. Edgerton, Harold A., and Donald G. Paterson. Table of standard errors and probable errors of percentages for varying numbers of cases. Journal of Applied Psychology, 10:378–91 (September, 1926).
16. Engel, Ernst. Lebenkosten belgischer Arbeiterfamilien früher und jetzt. Bulletin de l'Institut international de statistique, 9:1–124 (1895).
17. Fisher, M. L. Measured differences between problem and non-problem children in a public school system. Journal of Educational Sociology, 7:353–64 (1934).
18. Flemming, C. W., and S. A. Rutledge. The importance of the social and economic quality of the home for pupil guidance. Teachers College Record, 29:202–15 (Columbia University, 1927).
19. Francis, K. W. A study of the means of influence of socio-economic factors upon the personality of children. Journal of Juvenile Research, 17:70–77 (1933).
20. Garrett, Henry E. Statistics in psychology and education. Longmans, Green and Co., New York, 1926. 317 pp.
21. Goodenough, F. L., and J. E. Anderson. Experimental child study. The Century Co., New York, 1931.
22. Hartshorne, Hugh, and Mark A. May. Studies in the nature of character. Vol. I. Studies in deceit. The Macmillan Co., New York, 1928. 3 vols.

23. Heilman, J. D. A revision of the Chapman-Sims socio-economic scale. Journal of Educational Research, 18:117–26 (1928).
24. Holley, Charles Elmer. The relationship between persistence in school and home conditions. University of Chicago Press, 1916. 119 pp.
25. Kelley, T. L. Statistical method. The Macmillan Co., New York, 1923. 390 pp.
26. Kornhauser, Arthur W. The economic standing of parents and the intelligence of their children. Journal of Educational Psychology, 9:159–64 (1918).
27. Likert, Rensis. A technique for the measurement of attitudes (Archives of Psychology, No. 140). Columbia University, 1932.
28. McCormick, Mary Josephine. The measurement of home conditions (Social Science Monographs, Vol. I, No. 1). Washington, D. C., September, 1929. 23 pp.
29. ――――. A scale for measuring social adequacy (Social Science Monographs, Vol. I, No. 3). Washington, D. C., October, 1930. 73 pp.
30. Morgan, W. L., and A. M. Leahy. The cultural content of general interest magazines. Journal of Educational Psychology, 25:530–41 (October, 1934).
31. National Society for the Study of Education. Nature and nurture. Part I. Their influence on intelligence. Public School Publishing Co., Bloomington, Illinois, 1928. 465 pp.
32. Pearson, Karl B. On a new method of determining correlation between a measured character A and a character B, of which only the percentage of cases wherein B exceeds or falls short of a given intensity is recorded for each grade of A. Biometrika, 7:96–105 (1909).
33. Perry, Clarence Arthur. A measure of the manner of living. Quarterly Publications of the American Statistical Association, 13:398–403 (1913).
34. Sims, Verner Martin. The measurement of socio-economic status. Public School Publishing Co., Bloomington, Illinois, 1928. 33 pp.
35. Sydenstricker, Edgar. Economic status and the incidence of illness. Public Health Reports, 44:1821–33. United States Public Health Service, 1929.
36. Sydenstricker, Edgar, and Wilford I. King. The measurement of the relative economic status of families. Quarterly Publications of the American Statistical Association, 17:842–57 (1921).
37. ――――. A method of classifying families according to income in studies of disease prevalence. Public Health Reports, 35:2829–46. United States Public Health Service, November, 1920.
38. Symonds, Percival M. Diagnosing personality and conduct. The Century Co., New York, 1931. 601 pp.
39. Taussig, Frank W. Principles of economics. The Macmillan Co., New York, 1913. 2 vols.
40. Terman, Lewis M., and others. Genetic studies of genius. Vol. I. Mental and physical traits of a thousand gifted children. Stanford University Press, 1925. 648 pp.
41. Thomas, Coronal. Results of the Sims Socio-Economic Rating Scale when given to delinquent and non-delinquent juveniles. American Journal of Orthopsychiatry, 1:527–39 (October, 1931).
42. Thorndike, Edward L. An introduction to the theory of mental and social measurements. 3d ed., Teachers College, Columbia University, 1919. 271 pp.
43. Van Alstyne, Dorothy. The environment of three-year-old children: factors related to intelligence and vocabulary tests (Teachers College Contributions to Education, No. 366). Columbia University, 1929. 108 pp.
44. Williams, J. Harold. A scale for grading neighborhood conditions (Department of Research, Whittier State School, Bulletin No. 5). Whittier, California, 1917. 17 pp.
45. ――――. A guide to the grading of homes (Department of Research, Whittier State School, Bulletin No. 7). Whittier, California, 1918. 21 pp.
46. Yule, G. U. Introduction to the theory of statistics. J. B. Lippincott Co., Philadelphia, 1912.

SCHEDULES USED IN THE INVESTIGATION

Form. 4

UNIVERSITY OF MINNESOTA

INSTITUTE OF CHILD WELFARE

Serial No._____

THE CHILD AND HIS ENVIRONMENT

[Check in parentheses to indicate answer where choice is given, thus: (x)]

GENERAL INFORMATION

1. Name of field worker ....
2. Date of visit ....
3. Hour of day................A.M...............P.M..............
4. Name of family..
5. City or place..
   Street address ....
6. Telephone number ....
7. Size of community: less 1000 ( ); 1000-2500 ( ); 2500-10,000 ( ); 10,000-100,000 ( ); over 100,000 ( )
8. Person interviewed: mother ( ); father ( ); other..............
9. Is mother living: Yes ( ); No ( )
10. Is father living: Yes ( ); No ( )
11. Age of mother: ....
12. Age of father: ....
13. With whom is child living? both parents ( ); mother only ( ); father only ( ); father and stepmother ( ); mother and stepfather ( ); grandparents ( ); other
14. Is father sick? often ( ); occasionally ( ); seldom ( ); never ( ); nature of illness, if any?..............
15. Is mother gainfully employed? Yes ( ); No ( ) If so, at what?..............
16. Is mother sick? often ( ); occasionally ( ); seldom ( ); never ( ); nature of illness, if any?..............
17. Name of child..
18. Sex: Male ( ); Female ( )
19. Age................years...............months..............
20. Date of birth..
21. School grade...............School..............
22. Is child sick? often ( ); occasionally ( ); seldom ( ); never ( ); nature of illnesses, if any?..............

23. Has he had? infantile paralysis ( ); encephalitis ( ); epilepsy ( ); if none, check here ( )
24. Does he have a marked defect in? hearing ( ); sight ( ); speech ( ); if none, check here ( )
25. Does he have any special ability? Yes ( ); No ( ); if so, what ....
26. Is family known to any relief agency? Yes ( ); No ( )
27. How tall is the father?..............
28. How tall is the mother?..............
29. Physical measures of child: Height.............. Weight..............

REMARKS

....
....
....
....
....
....
....
....
....
....
....
....
....
....
....
....
....
....

CHILDREN IN FAMILY LIVING OR DEAD

(Put x after names of those dead. Do not include miscarriages.)

Name	Own child	Adopted child	Birthdate	Age	Sex	School grade	Employed

64

NEIGHBORHOOD

Score

.... 1. Are there stores in the same block with the home?
Y   N

.... 2. Is the home directly connected with a store? Y   N

.... 3. Are any of the following within one-fourth mile of the home?

Factories or warehouses	Y	N
Police station	Y	N
Pool hall	Y	N

CIVIL STATUS, EDUCATION, AND OCCUPATION

.... 4. Are parents separated or divorced? Y   N

.... 5. What was the highest grade completed by father?
0, 1, 2, 3, 4, 5, 6, 7, 8, 9, 10, 11, 12, 13, 14, 15, 16, 17, 18, 19, 20. Other..................

.... 6. What was highest grade completed by mother?
0, 1, 2, 3, 4, 5, 6, 7, 8, 9, 10, 11, 12, 13, 14, 15, 16, 17, 18, 19, 20. Other..................

.... 7. What is father's usual occupation?..........................

Minn. Scale I II III IV V VI VII

MATERIAL EQUIPMENT

.... 8. How many rooms?
Number: 1-2   2   4   5-7   8-10   over 10

.... 9. How many bedrooms?..........................

........10. How many people in the home?..........................

........11. How many persons per bedroom?
(Count two children under *ten* as one person)
3 or over; 2 but less than 3;
1 but less than 2; less than 1

........12. Do family rent home? Y   N

........13. Country or lake home? Y   N

........14. Is there any paid assistance in the home? Y   N
Number: 1 P.T. 2 P.T. 1 F.T. 2 F.T. 3 F.T. or more

........15. Are the following facilities provided?

Central Heating System	Y	N
Telephone	Y	N
Vacuum Cleaner	Y	N
Automobile	Y	N
A second automobile (not a truck)	Y	N
Radio	Y	N
Piano	Y	N
Ventilating fan for kitchen	Y	N
A second bathroom or more	Y	N
Washing Machine and Mangle	Y	N
Electric Refrigerator	Y	N
Folding camera	Y	N
Moving Picture Camera	Y	N
Playground equipment (2 pieces or more)	Y	N
Nursery or Recreational Room	Y	N
Boat	Y	N
Bicycle or tricycle	Y	N
Typewriter at home	Y	N
Fireplace	Y	N
Desk in living room	Y	N
Side wall, table, or floor lamps	Y	N

CULTURAL AND SOCIAL FACTORS

........16. How many daily papers are taken?
Number: 0   1   2   3 and over

Score

........17. Are any metropolitan papers other than the local papers taken? Y   N
If so, what?..........................

........18. How many magazines are regularly taken in the home?
Number: 0   1-2   3   4   5   6 or over

........19. What are the names of the magazines?..........................

....

....

....

....

....

....

....

........20. About how many children's books are in the home?
Number: 0   1-10   11-30   31-50   over 50

........21. About how many other books are in the home?
Number: 0   1-25   26-50   51-100   101-250   251-500 over 500

........22. Is there an encyclopedia? Y   N
If so, what?..........................

........23. Has father been a member of a

Professional club or scientific society	Y	N
Civic or political club	Y	N
Trade union	Y	N
P.T.A.	Y	N
Study club, literary or art society	Y	N
Fraternal	Y	N
Social club	Y	N
University Extension Course (2 or more courses)	Y	N
None ☐		

........24. Has mother been a member of a

Professional club or scientific society	Y	N
Civic or political club	Y	N
Trade union	Y	N
P.T.A.	Y	N
Study club, literary or art society	Y	N
Fraternal	Y	N
Social club	Y	N
University extension course (2 or more courses)	Y	N
None ☐		

........25. Do parents participate in any of the following forms of recreation?

Fishing or Hunting	Y	N
Bridge	Y	N
Tennis or Golf	Y	N
Horseback Riding	Y	N

........26. Has child had paid lessons outside of school in:

Music	Y	N
Dancing	Y	N
Art	Y	N
Expression or dramatics	Y	N
Languages	Y	N

........27. Has child been to dentist within past year? Y   N
If so, were teeth aching when taken? Y   N

........28. Did family go away for a vacation within the past year?
Y   N

........29. Does either parent play a musical instrument?
Y   N   If so, what?..........................

Indifferent, gave information grudgingly	Hesitant, after explanation gave information willingly	Very co-operative
Co-operation:		
1	2	3

University of Minnesota   Institute of Child Welfare

Serial No._____

THE CHILD AND HIS ENVIRONMENT
Interest Interview

I am going to ask you a few questions about things you like. It is not expected that you will like all the things I name, but that doesn't make any difference. I am asking a large number of boys and girls the same questions in order to learn what boys and girls everywhere like to do. You need not think long over any of them but try to answer every question correctly.

Age................ Grade........................

1. What are the names of the playmates you like best and how old are they?

Name	Age	Name	Age
a.		c.	
b.		d.	

2. *Here is a list of school studies. Read them carefully and *then* put a number 1 before the subject you like best; and a number 2 before the subject you like next best; and so on until all subjects have been numbered.

Arithmetic
Language
Social studies (History, geography, nature study, science)
Handwriting
Reading or literature
Spelling

(Do you like No. 1 best?)
* Omit for 1, 2, and 3 grades.

3. Here is another list of school studies. Read them carefully and *then* put a number 1 before the subject you like best; a number 2 before the subject you like next best and so on until all subjects have been numbered.

Cooking
Drawing
Gymnasium
Music
Manual training
Nature study

4. Did you go to a boys (or girls) camp this summer or the summer before last? Yes □; No □

5. (a) If so what is the name of the camp?

....

(b) How long did you stay there? 2 wks. or less □; 3 wks. □; 3-4 wks. □; 4-5 wks. □; 6 wks. or over □

6. Have you ever belonged to any paid clubs or groups? Yes□; No □

What are the names of your clubs?...........................

....
....
....
....
....
....
....

7. Have you been an officer in school, church, or club work? Yes □; No □ If so, what office?

....
....
....

None □

8. How many times have you gone to Sunday School in the last 4 weeks? 4 □; 3 □; 2 □; 1 □; none □

9. How many times did you go to the movies in the last 4 weeks?

....

Never □

10. Here is a list of the names of movies. Read them over and check the ones you have seen.

Abraham Lincoln	Ladies Man
Father's Son	Silent Enemy
Around the World Via the	The Single Sin
Graph Zep	Song O' My Heart
A Soldiers Plaything	The Run Around
At the Bottom of the World	Tom Sawyer
Man of the World	The Right of Way
My Past	With Byrd at the South Pole
Grumpy	The Beggars Opera
Young Sinners	The Great Meadow
Once a Gentleman	Dishonored
The Man in Possession	Parlor, Bedroom, and Bath
The Last Parade	The Conquering Horde
Rango	Drums of Jeopardy
Many a Slip	A Connecticut Yankee
Cimarron	Skippy
Chances	Kick In
Trader Horn	Daddy Long Legs
Born to Love	Ferry Tip Top
Three Who Loved	Pagliacci
Common Law	Goody Good
A Lady's Morals	The Millionaire
Shipmates	Paddy Pop

11. What do you usually do after school?...............
....
....

Is there any day of the week that you do something special?...........

12. How long do you usually study outside of school? 0-29 min. □; 30-59 min. □; over 60 min. □

13. What do you usually do on Saturday?...............
....

14. What books or magazines have you read this last 4 weeks just for the fun of it?

Books   Magazines

....
....
....
....
....
....
....
....
....

None ☐

15. Where do you get the books you read?
    a. Public library ☐
    b. School library ☐
    c. From other boys and girls ☐
    d. Own library ☐

16. Do you have a bank day at your school? Yes ☐; No ☐

17. Do you deposit money every time ☐; sometimes ☐; never ☐

18. Do you keep money in a small bank at home? Yes ☐; No ☐ In a real bank uptown? Yes ☐; No ☐

19. How do you get your money?
    a. Do you earn it? Yes ☐; No ☐; How..............

    b. Do your parents give it to you when you ask for it? Always ☐; once in a while ☐
    c. Do other people give you money when you don't earn it? Yes ☐; No ☐

20. Are you given a certain amount of money *regularly* to spend? Yes ☐; No ☐

21. What work would you like to do when you grow up?..............
....

Don't know ☐

22. *Are you collecting anything, just because you think it is fun to see what a large number you can save? (Response *Yes*, should be followed by *Tell me what you are saving.* Check and record number.)

Name	Name
Magazines	Pictures
Books	Flowers
Money	Insects
Stamps	Nests and Eggs
Stones	Electrical Apparatus
Glass	Time Tables
Phonograph Records	Marbles
Autographs	Labels and Coupons
Shells	Postcards
Bottle Tops (Milk, pop, etc.)	Curios
Buttons (political)	Street car transfers
Match boxes and folders	Other
Dolls	None

23. Name the things that you have made all by yourself in the last 4 weeks.
....
....

24. Name the things that you have made with others.
....
....

25. Suppose a fairy were to grant you three wishes, what would your wishes be?
1. ....
2. ....
3. ....

* Do not suggest answers.

INDEX